GETHSEMANE TO GOLGOTHA

40 BIBLE STUDY DEVOTIONALS
ABOUT JESUS' LAST DAY

BOBBY S. (BOB) TERRY

SONCOAST PUBLISHING

Gethsemane to Golgotha

Copyright © 2024 by Bobby Terry

ISBN 979-8-88758-021-0 Paperback

ISBN 979-8-88758-022-7 Ebook

All rights reserved.

No part of this book may be reproduced in any form or by any electronic or mechanical means, including information storage and retrieval systems, without written permission from the author, except for the use of brief quotations in a book review.

Scriptures taken from the Holy Bible, New International Version®, NIV®. Copyright © 1973, 1978, 1984, 2011 by Biblica, Inc.™ Used by permission of Zondervan. All rights reserved worldwide. www.zondervan.com The "NIV" and "New International Version" are trademarks registered in the United States Patent and Trademark Office by Biblica, Inc.™

Soncoast Publishing
PO Box 1504
Hartselle, AL 35640

www.soncoastpublishing.com

CONTENTS

Preface   v
Introduction   vii

1. The Spirit is Willing, but the Flesh is Weak — 1
2. When Silence is All We Get — 5
3. Jesus Was in Charge — 9
4. Even Judas Offered Forgiveness — 12
5. Bound Hand and Foot — 17
6. Finding Faithfulness — 21
7. How Different the Gardens — 25
8. A Dangerous Combination — 29
9. A Temple Not Made with Hands — 33
10. Are You the Christ? — 37
11. Blasphemy! — 41
12. Prophesy to us, Christ! — 45
13. Failure Doesn't Stop God's Caring — 49
14. Judas and Peter — 52
15. Alone — 56
16. He Opened Not His Mouth — 59
17. To Please the Crowd — 63
18. Jealousy and Zeal — 66
19. Who You Believe is Important — 69
20. Weighed and Found Wanting — 73
21. Unlikely Companions — 76
22. A Brief Encounter – Simon — 79
23. They Offered Him Wine — 83
24. They Do Not Know — 87
25. Two Thieves — 91
26. King of the Jews — 94
27. Gathered at the Cross — 97
28. Darkness — 101
29. "Not Yet" Doesn't Mean "Too Late" — 105
30. They Divided His Clothes — 109

31. Protesting Jesus' Death	112
32. The Ministry of Presence	115
33. I Commit My Spirit	119
34. The Curtain in the Temple	122
35. The Centurion's Confession	125
36. Who is Responsible?	129
37. Not an Accidental Death	132
38. More on Who Is Responsible for Jesus' Death	136
39. Witnesses to Jesus' Burial	140
40. Without Easter…	144
About the Author	149
Also by Bobby S. (Bob) Terry	151

PREFACE

Christianity teaches the Creator God broke into history at a particular time in a particular way for a particular purpose. So important was the event that history continues to be divided by this fulcrum point in time. Whether one uses the traditional "BC – AD" division (Before Christ and Year of our Lord in Latin) to mark time or the more current "BCE – CE" (Before the Common Era and Common Era), the fulcrum point balancing the two divisions remains the birth of Jesus of Nazareth. Christians believe that God broke into history when, "the Word (of God) became flesh and dwelt among us" (John 1:14). This Word was with God in the beginning and this Word was God, the Bible says. That is why Christians believe God became man and dwelt among us in Jesus.

Through Jesus, God sought to reconcile humanity to Himself, especially through Jesus' suffering sacrifice of himself as a sin offering for wayward humanity. That offering was a key element in God's plan to provide mankind a "way of escape" from the punishment of sin and access to eternal salvation.

Jesus' last day included the most public events of his ministry as well as his ultimate self-giving. While these devotionals reflect current

PREFACE

Biblical insights, their goal is to help readers reflect on the personal implications from the many incidents that make up what some call "the Passion of our Lord."

The study, prayer, conversations, and more that went into preparing these 40 devotionals based on Jesus' last day was a rewarding spiritual journey for me. I pray the results of that journey will be helpful to others.

INTRODUCTION

The choice to start these devotionals with the Garden of Gethsemane is more than an arbitrary decision. True, the story of Jesus' arrest, trials, and crucifixion is the longest and most detailed account of any experience of his life and that story begins in Gethsemane. It is also true that prior to the arrest, the Bible is clear that Jesus was in charge, choosing where he would go, what he would do, and with whom he would associate. But with the arrest in Gethsemane, it appears, at least on the surface, as if others were determining where Jesus went, what he did, and what happened to him. Most of the actors in the story failed to recognize the unseen hand of God directing the events so the prophecies of old about Israel's Messiah would be fulfilled.

The primary reason for starting with the Garden of Gethsemane is the dramatic change in tone as the disciples walked with Jesus from the Upper Room to his private place of prayer. The gospels of Matthew and Mark point this out most clearly. On that walk, Jesus told his followers, "This very night you will fall away from me" (Matthew 26:31; Mark 14:26). Jesus spoke of his death, his resurrection, and meeting the disciples again in Galilee.

INTRODUCTION

Imagine how that announcement changed the atmosphere of their brief journey. Only minutes before they had shared a meal, listened to Jesus' teachings, and worshipped together through singing. Now the disciples heard Jesus was about to die and they were about to forsake him. It was almost unbelievable.

Jesus' demeanor changed, too. The agony of what was about to happen became overwhelming. It increased with every step taking Jesus closer to the Garden. He told his inner circle of disciples his agony was "to the point of death." The agony would not end until Jesus breathed his last.

So, we begin this devotional journey as Jesus reaches the Garden of Gethsemane and we follow it all the way to what happened following the experience of Golgotha. Occasionally, certain information is repeated in a second devotional. This is to help each devotional stand on its own and not require information from a previous devotional for understanding.

I hope you find this devotional journey worthwhile. Blessings.

1

THE SPIRIT IS WILLING, BUT THE FLESH IS WEAK

"Watch and pray so that you will not fall into temptation. The spirit is willing, but the flesh is weak." Matthew 26:41

We have all heard references to this important passage. Often it is used as an excuse, something offered to justify failure. When Jesus spoke these words to his disciples in the Garden of Gethsemane, the statement was not given as an excuse but as a warning.

The Gospels of Matthew and Mark both describe Jesus strategically placing his disciples in two groups. The first he left near the entrance of the olive grove where he had gone to pray. He charged them to keep watch. Whether the disciples understood they were watching for one of their own - Judas Iscariot and a band of soldiers coming to arrest Jesus - is a matter of speculation.

Peter, James, and John – the leadership team of the disciples – Jesus took a little farther into the olive grove. Jesus also asked them to keep watch while he went off alone to pray.

The exact length of Jesus' prayer time is uncertain. Both gospel writers indicate it was about an hour. When Jesus finished the first of what would end up being three prayer sessions, he returned to his leadership team and found them asleep.

Jesus' response indicates surprise. Matthew quotes Jesus as asking, "Could you men not watch with me for one hour?" Again, he urged them to "watch," adding they should pray that they do not fall into temptation.

Then Jesus offered that famous statement, "The spirit is willing, but the flesh is weak."

The word spirit refers to the human spirit. In the Old Testament, it is that part of the human being that feels, thinks, and decides. Flesh is the tangible, perishable part of humanity.

Jesus said, "The spirit is willing." In 2 Chronicles 29:31 the word for "willing" means one trained and eager for service. Psalms 51:14 uses the word to describe one's spirit aligned with God's plan.

That is where the disciples thought they were. For three years they had followed Jesus and learned from him. Now they were ready to follow him into death. Earlier that evening Peter had sworn he would never betray Jesus "even if I have to die with you…" Overlooked, sometimes, are the next words in both Matthew and Mark – "and all the others said the same."

Evidently, all the remaining disciples had willing spirits.

"But the flesh is weak." Jesus did not say flesh was sinful. He said it was weak. It was perishable, vulnerable. The disciples' behavior illustrated that truth. They were asked to watch and pray but instead they slept. Their willing spirits were undermined by their weak flesh.

Some have asked if Jesus' words were just for the disciples or if the words might have voiced his own crisis. Though Jesus had been pointed toward the cross from the moment of his birth, Jesus had just spent about an hour asking God to "take away the cup," asking if there were not some other way to provide salvation for humankind.

Before the evening ended, he twice more prayed a similar prayer according to Matthew and Mark. Yet, each time he added "not my will but your will be done." Was this a time when for Jesus, the spirit was willing, but the flesh was weak?

Was his warning to the disciples tinged with understanding born out of personal experience?

The writer of Hebrews may offer guidance. In Hebrews 5:7 one reads, "During the days of Jesus' life on earth, he offered up prayers and petitions with loud cries and tears to the one who could save him from death." That seems to describe Jesus who was so overcome by sorrow in Gethsemane that he felt he was going to die.

The next verse says of Jesus, "Although he was a son, he learned obedience from what he suffered." Does that include Gethsemane where his sweat looked like drops of blood falling to the ground?

In Hebrews 4:15, the writer says, "For we do not have a high priest who is unable to sympathize with our weaknesses, but we have one who has been tempted in every way just as we are, yet without sin."

If Jesus' warning to the disciples is tinged with understanding from personal experience, then Jesus demonstrated the importance of prayer. In his struggles that night, he embraced "obedience unto death" through the power of prayer that overcame the weakness of flesh.

For Peter, James, and John it was a different outcome. They did not watch and pray and, despite their good intentions and willing spirits, they failed.

Hopefully all of us have willing spirits. We are trained and eager to serve our God according to his plans and purposes. Should we, also, heed the warning that our flesh is weak and vulnerable, and we can fail when trials cross our paths?

The only way to succeed is to watch and pray like Jesus asked of his disciples and like he himself did that night in the Garden of Gethsemane.

BOBBY S. (BOB) TERRY

Lord, help us to watch and pray so that we do not give in to temptation. Amen.

2

WHEN SILENCE IS ALL WE GET

"Abba, Father," he said, "everything is possible for you. Take this cup from me. Yet, not what I will, but what you will." Mark 14:36

Who among us has not gone to God in prayer pleading for some person, some cause, some outcome that was the center of our lives? I have.

And who among us has not been startled when our prayers to a loving and merciful God were answered with silence? Despite our sincerity, despite our earnestness, despite our certainty of God's power to affirm our requests, silence was the only response.

Jesus had a similar experience. In the Garden of Gethsemane, the night before his crucifixion, Jesus was practically overcome with the enormity of what lay before him. The Gospels of Matthew and Mark record Jesus saying he was so overcome with sorrow that he felt like he was going to die right then and right there.

Mark, believed to be the oldest gospel, says Jesus "fell to the ground" after walking a little distance from his disciples. Matthew is more descriptive. He writes that Jesus fell with his face buried in the dirt (Matthew 26:39). What parent's heart would not be opened by such pain in a child's life? What parent would not do everything possible to help that child?

Would God do any less?

Jesus boldly made his plea for God's help just like you and I have done. "Father," he prayed, "take this cup from me." That was the longing of his heart.

As Christian believers, we may be surprised at Jesus' prayer in Gethsemane. The Gospel of John relates Jesus predicting his death (12:23-28). There Jesus says his "soul is troubled" by his approaching death and questions if he should ask the Father to save him from this hour. "No," he answers, "it was for this very reason I came…" (v.27).

Some contend the horrendous suffering and death that awaited him motivated Jesus' prayer. Others argue it was the struggle between his human will and his divine will. More likely, it was the sinless Son of God becoming sin itself, as he paid the price for the sins of the world.

But the reason for the prayer is not the point. Whatever his motivation, Jesus prayed for deliverance.

In the same prayer, he acknowledged that the Father's will took precedence over his own. "Yet, not what I will but what you will," he prayed, according to Mark's account.

Because of the relationship between the Father and the Son, one would expect an answer. In John 12, mentioned above, when Jesus prayed that in his death the Father's name would be glorified (v. 28), God spoke saying, "I have glorified it and I will glorify it again."

That is the kind of response we long for when we offer our prayers to God. We want to hear from Him. We want Him to act.

But when Jesus prayed in the Garden of Gethsemane there was only silence. Matthew's and Mark's accounts say Jesus had three prayer seasons that night and that he repeated the same prayer each time (Matthew 26:44).

It must have been agonizing for Jesus. Luke says each time "he prayed more earnestly" and the sweat from his agony in prayer was like drops of blood falling to the ground. But nowhere – not Matthew, not Mark, not Luke – is there indication that God answered Jesus.

Yes, Luke says an angel came to comfort him. It is reminiscent of the time of temptation in the wilderness where, after Jesus vanquished Satan, angels ministered to Jesus. Perhaps Luke sees a comparison here. But Luke records no answer to Jesus' plea.

Our own experiences affirm that sometimes, in the midst of silence, God sends someone across our path to strengthen us. That person may not have answers, but they remind us that we are not alone, that God's Spirit is present, and so are God's people. They strengthen us for what lies ahead. And for that we are grateful.

Jesus bared his longing to God and he affirmed his trust in God. Doesn't that sound like us in those anguishing experiences of praying for loved ones, for ourselves, for churches, for the lost, and for the cause of Christ?

In Gethsemane, silence was the Father's answer and Jesus came to understand that through prayer. When Jesus finished his prayer time and returned to where his friends awaited him, they were all asleep. They had been unable to watch and pray as he had urged.

This time there was no scolding or disappointment as after the first and second prayer times. He told them to "sleep on." Jesus had worked through his crisis. He knew what lay before him. He always had. Now he was ready to face it.

Sometimes we know what is before us, too. We just have trouble accepting what we know is coming.

Look at Jesus. In silence the Father affirmed the reason Jesus came into the world – to give his life a ransom for many. Now as Jesus saw the parade of torches begin winding down from Mt. Zion toward where he waited, Jesus was ready. To the disciples he said, "Let us go," an imperative command. He marched purposely forward to drink the bitterest dregs from the "cup" that awaited him.

Silence doesn't mean that God is not present or that He doesn't hear us. It may be His answer.

So, when silence is all we get, maybe we should learn from it and prepare to walk forward certain of God's presence no matter what we face.

Lord, help us trust in you even during the silent times. Amen.

3

JESUS WAS IN CHARGE

"Jesus, knowing all that was going to happen to him, went out and asked them, 'Who is it you want?'" John 18:4

The Gospel of John recounts an unusual event related to the arrest of Jesus. Let's set the stage. In John 18:3, Judas appears guiding Roman soldiers to arrest Jesus. Like accounts in the other gospels, also with Judas were "officials of the high priests and Pharisees." But only John reports that Roman soldiers were included in the party sent to arrest Jesus.

The Greek describes the number of soldiers as a "cohort" which is one tenth of a Roman legion or between 500 – 600 soldiers. A Roman legion had about 5,000 soldiers plus a contingency of cavalry placing the number in a legion between 5,000 – 6,000 men under normal circumstances.

Many English translations opt to use other words to describe the size of the Roman contingency which accompanied Judas. Band, company, detachments, group – these are just some of the English words used to translate the Greek word for cohort.

If the Jewish authorities were given a full cohort of Roman soldiers to help arrest Jesus and those soldiers marched four abreast and took the most direct route from the Antonio Fortress where they were stationed to Gethsemane, then soldiers at the end of the marching line would have barely cleared the city walls before those at the head of the line reached the site where Jesus awaited them.

But it is not the size of the arresting party that is unusual. It is their reaction when Jesus confronted them. The Gospel of John never presents Jesus as a victim. He is always the victor. He is the one in charge. Verse four says Jesus went out to meet this group of people coming to arrest him. He initiated contact by asking, "Who is it you want?"

Notice verse 5. When the crowd said they sought Jesus of Nazareth, Jesus said, "I am he." Some scholars make much of the Greek words "ego emei" (I am he). The words are similar to the Greek name of God revealed to Moses at the burning bush in Exodus 3:14. There God's name is translated, "I am who I am." The writer of the Gospel of John may be trying to illustrate the power of the name of God when he reports, "When Jesus said, 'I am he,' they drew back and fell to the ground."

Imagine 500 or more Roman soldiers being flattened by the words of Jesus. And along with them, the officials of the high priests, the Temple police, Pharisees, and others were thrown to the ground, too. John is clearly showing that Jesus was in charge.

Jesus told those who had come to seize him to let the disciples go and they did, even after Peter cut off Malchus' ear (v. 10). To the whole crowd outside the gates of Gethsemane, Jesus asked, "Shall I not drink the cup the Father has given me?" Allowing himself to be arrested was his decision.

The Gospel of Matthew adds to this scene. When Peter struck the high priest's servant with the sword, Jesus ordered Peter to put the sword away, saying the Father would send twelve legions of angels to fight his cause, if Jesus asked (Matthew 26:53). The imagery is striking. If the attempt was to intimidate Jesus with the display of over-

GETHSEMANE TO GOLGOTHA

whelming force in a full cohort of Roman soldiers, it was a pitiful attempt. Jesus said 12 full legions of angels were at his disposal. That is 72,000 angels!

Historians report that in all of Syria and Palestine there were only six Roman legions at the time. And Jesus said twice that number was at his command. He was not intimidated by Roman military might or Jewish religious arrogance. Even if others did not understand, Jesus knew that he was in charge.

Even on the cross, Jesus was in charge. Through the torture, mockery, and rejection of the crucifixion, Jesus drank the last bitter dregs of the cup which, in Gethsemane, he said he had to drink. He did not call the 12 legions of angels. Instead, he was "pierced for our transgressions." He was "crushed for our iniquities." He was wounded that we might be healed. Like a sheep led to slaughter, "he opened not his mouth" (Isaiah 53:5, 7).

Through it all, Jesus was in charge as he became obedient even unto death.

Lord, help us to follow You, even when it leads us into suffering. Amen.

4

EVEN JUDAS OFFERED FORGIVENESS

"Jesus asked him 'Judas, are you betraying the Son of Man with a kiss?'" Luke 22:48.

The collusion between Judas and Jerusalem's religious leaders to kill Jesus is reported in all four gospels. Luke sets the timing of the scheme around Passover, the most important celebration of the Jewish religion. Matthew and Mark are more specific. They place the incident only two days before the Passover celebration.

While the chief priests, teachers, elders, and officers of the temple guard wanted Jesus dead, they did not want him killed during Passover. They feared the arrest of the charismatic Galilean might create a riot among the people (Matthew 26:5; Mark 14:2). Some say that during Passover, population of Jerusalem swelled from about 70,000 - 80,000 to more than a quarter of a million as worshippers from throughout the known world descended on the Judean city.

Days earlier, these pilgrims hailed Jesus as Messiah. The religious leaders wanted to seize Jesus secretively so the crowd would have no chance to rally to his support.

Surprisingly, Judas provided them that opportunity. Judas is identified as "one of the twelve," the closest followers of Jesus. This "one of the twelve" sought out the priests. Do not overlook the repeated references to Judas as "one of the twelve." Over and over again each writer emphasizes that Judas was a follower of Jesus, a disciple who had spent about three years following and learning from him. It is as if the authors want to drive home the boundless depth of betrayal involved in Judas' actions.

Left unexplained is how Judas knew about the Jewish plot to kill Jesus. How did he know to go to the chief priests, teachers, and elders to betray his leader? Was their plot common knowledge?

Some suggest the words of Jesus directed Judas. Matthew 26:2 quotes Jesus telling the disciples, "As you know, the Passover is two days away – and the Son of Man will be handed over to be crucified." But those words would have sent Judas to the Romans, for only they could put one to death by crucifixion.

Nor does the Bible share the reason for Judas' betrayal. Some believe he was disgusted by valuable perfume being poured over Jesus rather than being sold and proceeds used to help the poor (Matthew 26:6ff). Perhaps, but that is only one of several possible motives suggested by scholars.

Whatever the reason, the Bible affirms Judas agreed to sell out Jesus for 30 silver coins (Matthew 26:15).

The story moves rapidly after that. The next day, during what is commonly called The Last Supper, Jesus startled the disciples when he announced that one of them would betray him. The gospel of John describes the announcement more elegantly than the other gospels. There Jesus quotes Psalm 41:9 saying, "This is to fulfill the scripture, 'He who shares my bread has lifted up his heel against me.'"

Matthew and Mark put it more bluntly. Each quotes Jesus saying, "One of you will betray me."

Reactions of the disciples were almost predictable. They were both sad and indignant. According to Luke, they began talking among themselves about who would do such a thing. They ended up in a quarrel about who among them was the greatest – an issue that had plagued their fellowship for weeks.

One by one the disciples protested, "Surely not I," according to Matthew and Mark. But Judas' protest was different. Judas alone used the term "Rabbi" when he said, "Surely not I, Rabbi." Don't overlook that reference. Judas used it again a few hours later in the Garden of Gethsemane.

In Matthew 23, Jesus condemned religious leaders who liked to use titles such as "Rabbi" to build up their egos. In verse 8, Jesus forbade his disciples from using that title. Yet, here was Judas calling Jesus "Rabbi." To the casual reader, the title may seem unimportant, but to one who remembers the Lord's direction from the earlier incident, use of the term shows Judas already sat outside the fellowship of the disciples. Already, he disregarded Jesus' instructions.

To Judas' protest, Matthew has Jesus responding plainly, "Yes, it is you." In John, Judas is identified when Jesus gives him a piece of bread and instructs him, "What you are about to do, do quickly" (John 13:27).

Judas did act quickly. He went straight to the priests explaining the opportunity to seize Jesus secretly had come sooner than anticipated. What Judas offered was too good an opportunity to miss. Jesus would be at a private place outside the walls of Jerusalem. He could be arrested at night while most people slept. Jesus' fate could be sealed before anyone knew what was happening.

Judas came to Gethsemane leading a crowd sent by the chief priests to arrest Jesus. John says he also guided a detachment of soldiers. The one Judas kissed was to be arrested and led away to trial and whatever might follow.

Luke 7:45 presents the kiss as a sign of hospitality. Romans 16:16 pictures it as a sign of Christian fellowship. Evidently, Judas tried to appear as "disarmingly normal" as possible. But Jesus knew what Judas was about. Remember, hours earlier Jesus had confronted Judas about his treachery.

Just as there was irony in Judas using a sign of peace to betray Jesus, so there was irony in Jesus' response. Matthew has Jesus using a Greek word meaning "friend" but implying much more to address Judas. It is the same word used in Matthew 20:13 where the vineyard owner addressed complaining workers as "friends." The word is filled with sarcasm and implies something other than warm feelings.

Luke says Jesus stopped Judas before the actual kiss occurred (Luke 22:47ff). There Jesus called Judas by name, much like he called Peter by name in the Upper Room. Even though Jesus' heart must have been breaking to see one so close to him prepared to turn him over to his enemies, Jesus showed care for the one who approached.

"Judas are you betraying the Son of Man with a kiss," Jesus asked (v. 48). It was as if Jesus were saying "Judas, are you really going to do this?"

As he had done throughout his ministry, Jesus reached out to the sinner offering forgiveness. Jesus tried one final time to touch Judas' heart. The question was an implicit appeal to repent, even in the face of the foreknowledge of our Lord.

Luke says Satan had entered into Judas (Luke 22:3) and Judas would not be deterred. He betrayed Jesus. For doing so, his name became like a curse for the rest of history.

But do not overlook that at their final meeting, the Gospel of Luke shows Jesus reaching out to Judas offering opportunity to repent. Just as Jesus called Judas by name and offered him opportunity to repent, so Jesus offers us opportunity to repent. Whether we are modern day disciples who feel we have betrayed our Lord or one who has never trusted in His saving grace, Jesus reaches toward us offering forgiveness, no matter how vile our past, if we only repent.

The Bible promises "If we confess our sin, He (Jesus) is faithful and just to forgive our sin and to cleanse us from all unrighteousness" (1 John 1:9).

Lord, help us to come to you in confession and repentance for our sin. Amen.

5

BOUND HAND AND FOOT

> "Then the cohort of soldiers with its commander and the Jewish officials arrested Jesus. They bound him…" John 18:12

What an absurd scene it was. The Roman soldiers, together with temple guards, bound Jesus hand and foot after arresting him in the Garden of Gethsemane. Tradition says they tied his hands behind him and even put an iron chain around his neck.

They must have been really scared. Only moments earlier the words of the one now in chains had driven all the would-be captors to the ground (John 18:6). This sword-wielding, club-carrying mob of priests, scribes, soldiers, and guards had been met by a solitary figure who asked them whom they sought.

When the mob said they were looking for Jesus of Nazareth, Jesus announced "ego eimi" – I am he. Perhaps the most religious in the crowd caught the similarity to the name of God revealed in the story of Moses at the burning bush. When Moses asked God His name, God responded, "ego eimi" - I am who I am.

If the priests and scribes had understood Jesus' claim to deity in those worlds, it may have caused them to take a step backward, perhaps even to stumble. But no explanation other than the power of the words is available for why the hundreds who came to arrest Jesus were all driven back, stumbling and falling to the ground (John 18:6).

Jesus is, after all, the "Word made flesh" (John 1:4). His words healed the sick, fed the hungry, drove out demons, and opened spiritually blind eyes to the love of the eternal God. Perhaps the experience at Gethsemane was but a foretaste of what was to come. In 2 Thessalonians 2:8, the writer foretells of a time when "the lawless one" will be overthrown by the breath from the mouth of the Lord Jesus.

There was more to make the mob fearful. As they rose from their mishap, one of Jesus' followers – John's gospel says it was Peter – drew a sword and swung at the head of Malchus, a man who worked for the high priest. If seizing Jesus was the high priest's doing, as everyone expected, then Peter was going for the high priest's representative.

Malchus may have been quicker than Peter anticipated, for Peter's blade missed its target, but he did manage to cut off the man's ear. Peter's rash actions resulted in a scolding. Jesus told him to put away has sword and asked if Peter was trying to keep him from accomplishing the purpose for which he came. Then Jesus touched Malchus' ear and it was healed.

This was the man the mob was sent to arrest; a man who healed a wound with his touch; a man whose words drove them to the ground. No wonder they scurried to bind him before some other display of his power kept them from accomplishing their sinister purpose.

So here Jesus stood, bound and dragged along by a chain around his neck. Israel's history offers faint sounds of another whose enemies bound him hand and foot. The Philistines even gouged out Samson's eyes. They gloated at their triumph over their enemy much as the religious leaders gloated at binding Jesus in the dark of night. Before the people who had hailed Jesus with cries of "Hosanna" earlier in the week could rouse from their sleep, the scheme of the religious leaders would be carried out and Rome would crucify him.

Someone should have remembered that Samson got the last laugh. At the height of the Philistines' celebration of their victory, Samson pulled down the columns of the Philistine temple causing the whole structure to collapse. Judges 16:30 says Samson killed more Philistines in his death than he did during his entire life up to that point.

Jerusalem's religious elite may have scoffed at Jesus' claims. They had one more bind to wrap around him – death. Once in the grave, they would be rid of him forever. The only catch was to make sure he died at the hands of Rome as a criminal or seditionist and not from Jewish stones as a religious martyr.

How proud of themselves Caiaphas, Annas, and the others must have been as they watched their scheme unfold one event after the other. What they failed to notice was Jesus' words, "You have no power over me if it were not given to you from above" (John 19:11).

Ropes and chains were not the bonds that held Jesus that fateful night. He was bound by an eternal plan in place before creation itself, a plan to provide a way of escape for sinful humanity. It was the love of God that bound Jesus to the altar of sacrifice and atonement as "He became obedient…even unto death on the cross" (Phil. 2:8).

Jesus willingly went to his death as a sacrificial lamb for sinners declaring "no one takes my life from me, but I lay it down of my own accord" (John 10:18).

Not even death could bind Jesus, for just as he said that he laid down his life, he declared he would also take it up again. And he did.

As the sun began to rise on the Sunday following his crucifixion there was a great earthquake. The Roman guards watching the tomb once again fell to the earth quaking in fear and trembling. The stone blocking the entrance to Jesus' tomb rolled away, not to let Jesus out but to let humanity in. The empty grave testified that the bond on death itself was broken forever.

The Apostle Paul says Jesus "was declared with power to be the Son of God through the resurrection from the dead" (Rom. 1:4).

Jesus conquered sin and death. Jesus reigns as King of Kings and Lord of Lords. And he did it all because he was bound not by ropes and chains but by love to offer himself a sacrifice for all who believe on his name.

Lord, may your love bind us to you forever. Amen.

6

FINDING FAITHFULNESS

"Then all the disciples deserted him and fled." Matthew 26:57

Have you ever found yourself wondering what Jesus is doing in your life? Have you ever found yourself confused, even disappointed, with the way things are working out for you in the Lord's service? Have you ever found yourself expecting Jesus to do more than He seems to be doing?

All of us have. But we are not alone. So did his closest disciples.

For reasons lost in history, Peter, James, and his brother John made up the core leadership of the 12 disciples who followed Jesus during his three-year public ministry. Throughout the Gospel of Mark these three are chosen by Jesus to witness special events providing insights into who Jesus was and what He was about.

Mark 5:21ff tells the story of Jairus' daughter. Jairus was "a ruler of the synagogue." The Bible does not tell where the synagogue was, only that Jesus arrived "at the other side of the lake" (the Sea of Galilee) after casting out demons from a man in Gadara on the eastern shore.

Jairus forced himself through the large crowd gathered to greet Jesus. He pled with Jesus to hurry to his home where Jairus' 12-year-old daughter was near death. "Please come and put your hands on her so that she will be healed and live," he begged.

Mark says, "Jesus went with him" but before they reached the home, servants met them with the sad news of the young girl's death (v. 35). Jesus dismissed what the servants reported, urging Jairus not to be afraid but to believe.

If you were Jairus, or Peter, James, or John for that matter, you faced a dilemma. The servants knew when someone died, when their heart stopped, and breathing ceased. That is what happened to the child. But Jesus insisted she was only sleeping.

The crowd laughed at Jesus' words. But what would her father do? What would the disciples do?

Jesus did not allow anyone into the room where Jairus' daughter lay except Peter, James, and John. With them as witnesses, he touched her hand and said, "Little girl, I say to you, get up." And miracle of miracles, she did.

Peter, James, and John, along with others, had seen Jesus command the forces of nature when He calmed a storm the night before (Mark 4). They had seen him triumph over demons in Gadara and heal a woman of a disease that plagued her for 12 years. Now the three stood alone with Jesus and saw his power command death itself.

In Mark 9, Peter, James, and John are again chosen by Jesus for a special experience. They accompanied him up a "high mountain" for what is called the "transfiguration." The three leaders of the disciples saw persons they instinctively recognized as Moses and Elijah at Jesus side. On one side stood Moses representing the Jewish law. On the other side stood prophecy in the form of Elijah. In between was the grace of God in the person of Jesus.

Jesus began to glow with dazzling white light the disciples could not understand or explain. It was as if the glory of God were visible in the person of Jesus. Mark's gospel says law and prophecy slipped away. Only the grace of God remained - Jesus.

Peter, James, and John glimpsed the glory of God in Jesus, even if they did not fully understand what they saw.

On the night before his crucifixion, Jesus went to Gethsemane, a place he frequented for prayer. His "hour" was near, and he needed time alone with his Heavenly Father. Still, he longed for human companionship as death approached.

Jesus asked all the disciples to watch while he prayed. But he took Peter, James and John a little farther into the olive grove and, in a rare moment, shared his sorrow. "My soul is overwhelmed with sorrow to the point of death," he confessed (Mark 14:34). He asked his closest earthly friends - these core leaders - to watch and pray with him.

Instead, Peter, James, and John fell asleep. Even a second request by Jesus could not keep them awake. As Jesus endured his worst moments of human agony, as He learned "obedience even unto death," his closest friends could not watch and pray as he asked.

Peter, James, and John. They saw the power of Jesus over disease and death and somehow did not understand it. They saw the glory of Jesus in the transfiguration but missed its implications. They were invited to support Jesus in his agony but slept.

And when Jesus was arrested, Mark says, "Everyone deserted him and fled," even Peter, James, and John (Mark 14:50). Talk about confusion, disappointment, and broken dreams.

Thankfully, that was not the final word. In time, confusion gave way to insight. Disappointment turned to amazement. New visions replaced broken dreams. Those who once fled in fear became pillars of the Christian church honored through the ages for the faithfulness.

The reason for the change? There were many, but one was that Peter, James, and John did not choose isolation or separation amidst their confusion, doubt, disappointment, and failures. They held on to Jesus and to one another. And Jesus held on to them, providing new revelations and understanding that transformed their lives.

When the three disciples thought their journey with Jesus was ending, it was only just beginning.

Being pillars of the church may be "a bridge too far" for most of us. But if we stay with Jesus and stay with his church, we will at least travel the same road as Peter, James, and John. We will not be lost in confusion, doubt, disappointment, and failure. Instead, we will find faithfulness and all that it brings.

Lord, help us faithfully love you and follow you with all our heart, soul, mind, and strength. Amen.

7

HOW DIFFERENT THE GARDENS

"Then Jesus went with his disciples to a place called Gethsemane."
Matthew 26:36

One was an idyllic place, the other probably an olive grove. One garden was planted by God Himself, according to Genesis 2:8; the other by a family of farmers who eked out a living pressing olives into oil.

One garden's location is unknown. The Bible says only it was planted "toward the east in Eden." It must have been a beautiful place. The writer of Genesis says it contained "every tree that is pleasing to the sight and good for food." The garden was watered by a river system that included the great Tigris and Euphrates.

There God placed humanity, giving dominion over all creation. And there God offered Himself in fellowship with that part of creation He called "very good."

Only a small stream flowed near the second garden — the Kidron Brook. Over the centuries it had been a place of cleansing. First Kings 15:13 reports that at the Kidron Brook, Asa burnt "an abominable image for Asherah" which Maacah, his mother, had set up.

In the reforms of Hezekiah, "all the uncleanness found in the temple of Yahweh" was cast into the Kidron Brook by the Levites (2 Chron. 29:16).

Later, King Josiah brought all the pagan idols in Jerusalem to the Kidron Brook to be burnt and smashed into dust.

The second garden was located along the eastern edge of this little brook at the base of the Mount of Olives. Crossing the Kidron was considered the gateway to the wilderness, providing a hint of what the area was like. It was mostly dry and brown, watered by runoff captured in large cisterns during the rainy season. It was not lush and verdant like the first.

Eden was the name of the first garden. The second garden is known as Gethsemane. To each of these special places came one the Bible calls Adam.

In Eden, Adam and his wife, Eve, lived in harmony with creation and with the Creator, but that all changed when the serpent described God as envious and unreliable (Gen. 3:1–9). God did not want their eyes to be open to the insights He alone possessed, said the serpent. And the serpent's lies about God grew bolder with each word. God did not want them to know what He knew or understand what He understood, said the serpent.

God was the enemy and could not be trusted, claimed this agent of evil and temptation.

In Gethsemane, temptation came to the One called the Second Adam — Jesus of Nazareth. It was not their first encounter. Three years earlier Satan had tempted Jesus, but each time Jesus rejected the invitation to selfishness in order to be obedient to God.

Now the tempter was back. On the night before his crucifixion, as Jesus looked at what lay before him and said, "Let this cup pass from me" (Luke 22:42). So intense was his struggle that Jesus told friends he felt like he was going to die right then and there. His choice was to save himself or to save others.

In Eden, the first Adam concluded God could not be trusted. In rebellious defiance, Adam tried to take that to which he was not entitled. He wanted to be like God. Adam ate the forbidden fruit.

In Gethsemane the Second Adam added to his prayer, "Yet not my will but Thine be done." The Second Adam would be obedient, even unto death.

Ironically, the selfish grasping of the first Adam's rebellion brought sin, condemnation, and death into the world. The selfless giving of the Second Adam provided forgiveness, reconciliation, and life.

The writer of 1 John reflects on the story of the two Adams and concludes, "For all that is in the world, lust of the flesh and the lust of the eyes and the boastful pride of life is not from the Father but is from the world. And the world is passing away, and also its lusts, but the one who does the will of God abides forever" (1 John 2:16–17).

The Apostle Paul comments on the differences between the two Adams when he writes in Philippians 2:6 that "Christ Jesus, who, although He existed in the form of God, did not regard equality with God a thing to be grasped."

As a result of Jesus' faithful obedience, God offers mankind something to which he has no right — forgiveness of sin.

In Eden, shame and guilt were the inevitable result of disobedience. When God looked for Adam, Adam hid among the trees. Gone was the joy of fellowship with the Provider. Instead, Adam hid his body behind fig leaves and himself behind anything that might keep him from God.

Gethsemane was a different story. In the distance, Jesus could see the burning torches of a band of men winding down the road from Mount Zion. He knew they were coming for him. But the Second Adam was not driven by fear or shame. He would not run or hide like the first Adam.

Instead, Jesus greeted those who came to arrest him with an almost satirical question, "whom do you seek," for Jesus knew the answer.

He knew all things. Before Jesus stood an array of ecclesiastical and civil power, but Jesus was still in charge. No one would take His life, but Jesus would give His life as a ransom for many.

From Eden, the first Adam walked into history the victim of sin, a disobedient transgressor condemned to death. Because of him (and Eve), all humankind is destined to walk a similar path of transgression and trespass against the will of God. As the Bible teaches, "All have sinned and come short of the glory of God" (Rom. 3:23).

From Gethsemane the Second Adam left in chains, but none call Him victim. Jesus left as victor. His obedience to God conquered death and the grave. His selfless sacrifice opened the door for a new humanity formed through faith in Jesus.

The Garden of Eden shows Adam's act of selfishness. The Garden of Gethsemane shows the Second Adam's act of mercy. Eden ended with condemnation. Gethsemane opened the door to forgiveness. Eden resulted in death. Gethsemane was the beginning of life for all who believe "that God so loved the world that He gave His one and only son that whoever believes in him should not perish but have eternal life" (John 3:16).

Thank you, Lord, for Jesus. Amen.

8

A DANGEROUS COMBINATION

"The chief priests and the whole Sanhedrin were looking for evidence against Jesus so they could put him to death." Mark 14:55

Mention the Sanhedrin to a Christian and one is likely to get a negative reaction. In the gospel accounts of Jesus' arrest, trials, and crucifixion, members of the Sanhedrin are the bad guys. For example, Mark 14:55 says, "The chief priests and the whole Sanhedrin were looking for evidence against Jesus so they could put him to death...."

Many Christians think of the Sanhedrin as hypocritical religious leaders concerned with their own welfare. Religiously, they are seen as ultra-legalists. Politically, they were governed by self-interest.

Historically, violence against a religious rival was not unusual in Jesus' day. One historian writes, "Irrefutably, Jews hated and killed one another over religious issues between 130 BC and 70 AD."

Still, it is appropriate to ask if every member of the Sanhedrin was a hypocritical religious leader or were some driven by other motives?

Consider the story of Saul of Tarsus. We know him better as Paul the Apostle. In Acts 22, Paul says he persecuted Christians "to their death" because he was "zealous for God" (vv. 4-5). Paul did not consider himself a hypocritical religious leader. His motivation was being zealous for God.

Might some of the Sanhedrin have felt the same way?

Sometimes Christians forget that Moses instructed that certain prophets should be put to death. Deuteronomy 18:20 says, "But a prophet who presumes to speak in my name anything I have not commanded him to say…must be put to death." Even if the prophet does "miraculous signs or wonders" but "preaches rebellion against the Lord your God" that prophet must be put to death (Deut. 13:1-2).

Imagine the zealous Jew's reaction when Jesus belittled the Pharisee who strove to keep religious commandments. He prayed regularly, gave to religious causes, and observed the practices of personal piety. Yet, this man was condemned by Jesus while the tax collector was praised (Luke 18:11ff).

And Jesus openly associated with notorious public sinners, something a God-fearing Jewish person would not do.

Perhaps more importantly, Jesus claimed he could speak for God on his own authority.

To the pious Pharisee, Jesus' concept of himself, his teachings, and his conduct all violated the teachings of the faith passed down through the centuries. The obvious conclusion was that Jesus presumed to speak in God's name things that God had not commanded. That made him worthy of death.

Not to be forgotten is the origin of the Pharisees. Pharisees believed Israel failed and God allowed the nation to go into captivity because the Jews did not follow the law. That was a mistake that would not be made again.

While the Sadducees followed the laws of Moses, the Pharisees sought to understand the implications of the law so they could keep it down to the smallest details. They would brook no violation of the teachings of their faith because to do so was to risk destruction and prevent the reestablishment of the nation of Israel.

Like Saul of Tarsus, they may have opposed Jesus out of zealousness for God. They were so committed to preserving what they had inherited, they could not imagine God doing anything different in the present.

Perhaps some of us are still like that.

Caiaphas's motivation may not have been so pure. He was the High Priest and leader of the Sanhedrin. History tells us Caiaphas was first appointed to the office in 18 A.D. by Valerius Gratus, Rome's representative at the time. When Pontius Pilate succeeded Gratus in 26 AD, Caiaphas was kept on. Altogether, Caiaphas served 19 years as High Priest.

Since Rome preferred to rule through local surrogates, the Jewish High Priest was the person in charge of Jerusalem, accountable only to the Roman governor.

Caiaphas was a capable man and an astute politician. His comment in John 11:47 provides insight into his thinking about Jesus. Caiaphas feared the power of Jesus if left unchecked. He concluded, "If we let him go on like this, everyone will believe in him and then the Romans will come and take away both our place and our nation" (John 11:48).

Caiaphas' concern was political, a concern for the nation's well-being. He was also concerned about "our place." Was that a reference to the Temple or to the position of leadership which he held and the leadership of other members of the Sanhedrin?

Caiaphas told Sanhedrin members it was better for one man to die for the nation rather than the whole nation perish (John 11:50). His words manipulated a religious issue into a political emergency.

Later Caiaphas called Jesus a threat to Rome. Hear Caiaphas and others attempt to back Pilate into a corner by saying, "If you let this man go, you are no friend of Caesar. Anyone who claims to be a king opposes Caesar." Hear Caiaphas' shout, "We have no king but Caesar."

First the Sanhedrin. Then the Roman governor. Both fell to the High Priest's manipulation. To one, Caiaphas said Jesus was a threat to religious faithfulness. To the other, he said Jesus was a threat to political stability. Caiaphas got his way through manipulation, deceit, breaking the rules, lies, misuse of power, and more.

Some still practice the ways of Caiaphas and some still allow themselves to be manipulated as easily as did the Sanhedrin and Pilate. Both are wrong.

When these two ingredients are combined - the manipulation of leaders motivated by self-interest and the sincere efforts of people zealously trying to please God - it can be a dangerous combination.

Lord, guard us against allowing our zeal for You to be co-opted for selfish causes by others. Amen.

9

A TEMPLE NOT MADE WITH HANDS

"I tell you that one greater than the temple is here," Matthew 12:6

For Bible-believing Christians, it can be confusing when one passage of Scripture seems at odds with another passage. Take, for example, the passage in Mark 14:53ff where Jesus appears before the Sanhedrin following his arrest in Gethsemane.

Mark says clearly, "Then some stood up and gave this false testimony against him: 'We heard him say I will destroy this man-made temple and in three days will build another not made by man'" (vv. 57-58). That passage seems to say that any charge against Jesus that he would destroy the temple in Jerusalem and replace it with one not made by human hands is false.

Yet, in John 2:19, in response to a demand for a sign of his authority, Jesus told Jewish leaders, "Destroy this temple and I will raise it again in three days."

In Matthew's account of Jesus' trial before the Sanhedrin, witnesses against Jesus made similar charges related to the temple but nothing is said about them being false. "This fellow said, 'I am able to destroy the temple of God and rebuild it in three days'" (Matthew 26:61).

Even the writer of Mark shows Jesus foretelling the destruction of the Jerusalem temple. As Jesus and his disciples left the temple area, Jesus said, "Do you see all these great buildings? Not one stone here will be left on another; every one will be thrown down" (Mark 13:2).

So, if Jesus had predicted the destruction of the temple and had promised to "raise it again in three days" as John reports, why does Mark call the testimony of the witnesses false in Mark 14:57? Why does Matthew include similar comments but allows them to stand unchallenged?

Scholars have sought to answer that question for years and several different possibilities have been offered. Some point out that Jesus never said "I will destroy" as reported by the witnesses in Mark. In John 2, the ones who would destroy the temple were the Jews. In essence, there Jesus said if you destroy this temple, I will raise it again in three days.

Two verses later the writer of John's gospel makes it clear that Jesus spoke about the temple of his body and not the Jerusalem temple. That difference may have been missed by the crowd.

In Mark 13, no particular force is identified behind the promised destruction of the temple. From our point in history, we look back and know it was the Romans who tore down the temple in 70 AD and "not one stone was left on another."

So, when Mark's witnesses said Jesus promised to personally destroy the temple, it was false testimony.

Some scholars point to the commentary about Mark's witnesses not agreeing with one another (Mark 15:59) and conclude that one witness said he had heard Jesus threaten to destroy the temple and the other said he heard Jesus say he would rebuild it in three days. Given that it took Herod 46 years to build the temple and the temple mount, that would be quite a feat.

An explanation embraced by all for Mark calling the witnesses' testimony false may never be found, but the result of their testimony is clear. The Sanhedrin could not convict Jesus of threats to the temple because the two witnesses did not offer collaborating testimony, a requirement under Jewish law.

Mark's description of Jesus' trial before the Sanhedrin carefully outlines the two great concerns of the Jews. The first was the threat to the temple, the heart of Jewish faith and identity. The second was the threat this Galilean outsider posed to the Jewish leaders themselves.

Stymied by the inability to convict Jesus on threatening the temple, Caiaphas, the high priest, had to abandon that line of questioning and focus on the second.

"Are you the Christ, the son of the Blessed One?" he asked (v. 61).

When Jesus answered, "I am," Caiaphas and the Sanhedrin had what they sought – evidence to convict Jesus. They considered Jesus' words blasphemy and Jesus a false prophet deserving death.

Mark continues these two great concerns as he describes the reactions of the crowd to Jesus' crucifixion. In Mark 15:29-30, those in the crowd taunt him about his ability to destroy the temple but being unable to save himself. Evidently, Jesus' statements about the temple's destruction had been widely circulated.

The other taunt comes from the "chief priests and teachers of the law," members of the Sanhedrin. They mocked Jesus for claiming to be the promised Messiah (vv. 31-32).

Sometimes overlooked is that Mark also ends chapter 15 with these same two issues. After Jesus "breathes his last," the veil separating the Holy of Holies from the rest of the Jewish temple was torn in two from top to bottom (v. 38).

For centuries, Jewish high priests had gone into the Holy of Holies to offer sacrifices for their own sins and then the sins of others. But by the law nothing was made perfect (Hebrews 7:19). Now a better hope was introduced. Jesus sacrificed for the sins of all when he offered himself a once for all atonement for sin (v. 27). Now he and he alone was able to save completely those who come to God through faith in him (v. 25).

It would be another 40 years before Roman General Titus physically destroyed the Jerusalem temple, but the heart and hope of the temple died the moment Jesus breathed his last.

Three days later when Jesus rose from the dead, all who dared to see would understand. Jesus was not only the site of the sacrifice; he also was the one offering the sacrifice and he was the sacrifice. As affirmed in Matthew 12:6, he was "greater than the temple…."

> *Jesus - Son of God, a temple not made with hands, offering forgiveness to all who come to God through him. Thank you, Lord. Amen.*

10

ARE YOU THE CHRIST?

"So the holy one to be born will be called he Son of God." Luke 1:35

Careful readers of Scripture know the synoptic gospels – Matthew, Mark, and Luke – present slightly different accounts of Jesus' trial before the Sanhedrin. One difference is who posed the important question about Jesus being the Christ, the Son of God.

Matthew and Mark both put the question in the mouth of Caiaphas, the Jewish High Priest. Luke says the question was put by the Sanhedrin as a whole. The Sanhedrin was a council composed of the chief priests of the temple, teachers of the law, and elders of the people. It was led by "the High Priest" who was appointed by Rome.

There are also differences in the question. Matthew has the High Priest giving a directive, "Tell us if you are the Christ, the Son of God" (Matthew 26:63). In Mark, the High Priest poses a question and uses a descriptive to identify God, "Are you the Christ, the Son of the Blessed One?" (Mark 14:61). Luke also uses a question but omits a reference to Jesus being the Christ. "Are you then the Son of God?" the council asks (Luke 22:70).

The gospel writers also present Jesus as giving slightly different answers to the queries. And the different accounts of his answer have created some confusion.

Mark presents the most direct answer. In Mark 14:62, Jesus declares, "I am" when asked if he were the Christ, the Son of God. It was a straightforward answer that no one could misunderstand. It was an answer that put an exclamation point behind earlier accounts in Mark's gospel about who Jesus was. In Mark 8:29, Peter confessed, "You are the Christ." In Mark 9:7, God speaks out of a cloud saying, "This is my Son whom I love."

Now when Caiaphas asked Jesus if he is the Christ, the Son of the Blessed One, Jesus boldly declared, "I am." Jesus understood himself to be God's son and he understood his role to be that of the Christ, the Greek form of the Hebrew word meaning Messiah.

Earlier in Mark's story, Jesus had commanded unclean spirits not to tell anyone who he was (Mark 3:11). He also told his disciples not to share with others Peter's confession that he was the Christ (Mark 8:30). But now there was no need for caution. Now the wheels of redemption's story were rolling and soon everyone would witness signs pointing to Jesus as the Son of God.

Jesus added, "You will see the Son of Man sitting at the right hand of the Mighty One and coming on the clouds of heaven." Because the English language uses the same word for "you singular" as it does for "you plural," English readers often miss this point. The Greek uses the plural form of you in this verse, so everyone knows Jesus is not talking just to Caiaphas but to the whole Sanhedrin.

It is as if Jesus is driving the point home with a hammer. I am the Son of God, he said. What's more, you will see me sitting at the right hand of God Himself and you will see my power when I return on the clouds of the sky.

Could Jesus have answered the question more clearly?

Matthew has Jesus giving a more nuanced answer. Instead of a straightforward response to the question about being the Christ, the Son of God, Jesus replied, "You have said it" (Matthew 26:64). The answer was not a "yes" or "no" response.

Some people who have trouble with Jesus being the Son of God frequently point to this verse. They claim that when Jesus said, "You have said it," he refused to accept the claims made for him by his followers – that he was the Christ, the Son of God. Jesus' answer was an attempt to distance himself from their claims, the argument goes.

For centuries Biblical interpreters have wrestled with the question of whether Jesus was embracing the identity of the son of God by putting that confession on Caiaphas' lips or if he was rejecting it saying that is what you say about me, but I don't say it about myself.

Help with that question is provided earlier in this same chapter. In verse 23 Jesus tells the disciples that one of them will betray him. In verse 25, Judas says, "Surely not I, Rabbi." Jesus responds with the same Greek words used in verse 64 and translated both places as "You have said it."

Jesus' reply to Judas was a positive response. "You have said it." Unintentionally, Judas had confessed his intended evil. The truth fell from his own lips. Likewise, Caiaphas' question confessed the truth he did not want to acknowledge. Here the "you" is singular, and Jesus responded that the Jewish High Priest himself - the one who led the effort to take his life - had confessed the truth that Jesus was the Christ, the Son of God.

Luke's account of the incident is a little different than either Matthew or Mark. Luke separates the question of Matthew and Mark into two questions. The first is the demand to tell them if he is the Christ. To that inquiry Jesus says, "If I tell you, you will not believe" (Luke 22:68). Jesus does not answer the question directly, but he does declare that all will see him sitting at the right hand of the Father and coming on the clouds.

Every member of the Sanhedrin understood that Jesus was claiming to be the Christ, even without a yes or no answer to their question.

That prompted the second inquiry, "Are you then the Son of God?" (v. 70). Jesus replied, "You say that I am." Although the Greek words are slightly different, Luke does the same thing as Matthew. He turns the words of the whole Sanhedrin back on them. In Matthew, it was Caiaphas' words that Jesus turned into, "You yourself have said that I am the Son of God." Here it is the words of the greatest council in Judaism that Jesus turns into, "You yourself say that I am the Son of God."

One scholar observed that Luke began his gospel with an angelic announcement that Jesus will be called "the Son of God" (Luke 1:35). And here on the last day of Jesus' earthly life, the whole Sanhedrin joins the angel Gabriel in declaring that Jesus is the Son of God.

Yes, there are slight differences in the way each gospel writer recounts the story of Jesus before the Sanhedrin, but there is essential unity in Jesus' response. In all three gospels Jesus clearly embraces his role as the Christ and his identity as the Son of God.

Thank you, Lord, for sending your Son Jesus to be our savior. Amen.

11

BLASPHEMY!

"Then the high priest tore his clothes and said, 'He has spoken blasphemy! Why do we need any more witnesses?'" Matthew 26:65

"Blasphemy!" That was the unanimous decision of Jewish officials to Jesus' claim that he was "the Christ, the Son of God," made during the spiteful interrogation following his arrest. In the gospels of Mathew and Mark, it is Caiaphas, the ruling High Priest, who called the answer blasphemy. In Luke's gospel, the whole Sanhedrin council considered Jesus' answer worthy of death. The word blasphemy is not used in Luke but there is no mistaking the Sanhedrin's conclusion.

But what is blasphemy?

Scholarly books examine the term carefully in sacred and secular writings of the time. Some even count the number of times the term is used by Jewish historian Josephus and Philo, a Roman historian, and try to determine the meaning in each usage.

One unanimous conclusion is the charge was serious. Records from the first century show people being put to death after being convicted of blasphemy.

In general terms, blasphemy was claiming for oneself what belonged to God or belittling or insulting one who deserved respect – God or one of the prophets such as Moses.

Jesus faced this charge most of his ministry. Mark 2 begins with the story of Jesus healing the paraplegic. In verse 5, Jesus says to the paraplegic, "Son, your sins are forgiven." Notice the reaction of the "teachers of the law." They called the words blasphemy saying, "only God can forgive sin" (v. 7). They saw Jesus claiming for himself something that belonged to God alone.

In John 8:58-59 Jesus claimed, "Before Abraham was, I am." The reaction of the crowd was to take up stones to kill Jesus for what they considered blasphemy. The same is true in John 10:30 where Jesus declared, "I and my Father are one."

Each time Jesus challenged the teachings of Moses with his series of "You have heard it said…but I say to you" statements, he opened himself to charges of blasphemy. His actions indicated he was greater than Moses, the greatest of Jewish prophets, and able to change Moses' teachings.

Even Jesus' statements about being able to destroy the temple and build it back in three days was considered blasphemy by the Jews. The temple was God's house, and it was insulting to God to claim the power to destroy and rebuild God's house.

Every reference to Jesus as the Christ or Messiah, the special Son of Man or Son of God, was arrogant blasphemy to Jewish leaders. That is one of the reasons the people of Nazareth attempted to kill Jesus when he announced his public ministry in the synagogue (Luke 4). Residents understood this son of Joseph to be claiming something for himself that could not possibly be true. It was blasphemy.

Information about Jesus' blasphemous acts was mostly hearsay for Caiaphas and members of the Sanhedrin. The synoptic gospels show little interaction between Jesus and Jerusalem officials before Jesus' final trip to Judah's capitol city. But here Jesus was standing before them. Then he responded to their most important question, "Are you the Christ, the Son of God?"

All three synoptic writings report Jesus telling his jurors they would see him sitting at the right hand of God. Now there could be no question what Jesus thought about his relationship to the Father. With their own ears they had heard Jesus say they would see him coming in the clouds in judgment. There could be no doubt about Jesus' claim to power and authority.

"Blasphemy," they declared. This uneducated, untrained hick from the rural village of Nazareth in Galilee was claiming for himself what clearly belonged to God alone. Jesus' claims insulted God, Moses, and the Jewish nation. According to the law, he deserved to die, they concluded.

No longer did they have to worry about secondhand reports. Jesus had boldly declared these beliefs in their presence. Again, no longer was there any doubt about this man's crimes.

But arrogance, false claims, and insults can work two ways. The Bible says the Jewish leaders were guilty of blaspheming against Jesus. That point is made in the King James translation of Luke 22:65 where it reads, "And many other things blasphemously spake they against him (Jesus)." Blasphemy is also referenced in the New American Standard Bible and several others.

Unfortunately, some English versions use terms like "insult" or "revile" to translate the Greek word for blasphemy. When that happens, the reader can miss the point that Matthew, Mark, and Luke thought Jewish authorities blasphemed against Jesus. They did so when they commanded Jesus to prophesy before his trial (Luke 22:64). They did so when the High Priest stood at the base of the cross and mocked that Jesus could save others but not himself (Mark 15:31). They did so when the crowd taunted about his ability to destroy the temple and build it back, but he could not come down from the cross (Matthew 27:38-39).

It is not too much of an overstatement to say the separation of early Jewish Christian from the Jewish community was over the issue of blasphemy. For Christians, Jesus was not another rabbi debating the teaching of Scripture. He was the Christ (Messiah). He was the longed-for Son of Man. He was the Son of God. He was Savior.

Each claim sounded like blasphemy to the Jews. But when the Jews denied these truths, it was blasphemy on their part to Christians. The result was two separate communities to this day with each considering the other guilty of blasphemy.

Today there are signs that people are increasingly turning away from the historical confessions of the Christian faith. Some deny that Jesus ever lived, that he is the Son of God and Savior of all who call upon him in believing faith. Like Caiaphas and members of the Sanhedrin, they blaspheme our Lord with their insults, false claims, and disbelief.

And like the first Christians, individual believers and the church as a whole respond to their blasphemy with faithful proclamation that Jesus in the Christ, God's unique son, Savior of all who will believe.

Lord, may we faithfully share that 'God was in Christ reconciling the world to Himself.' Amen.

12

PROPHESY TO US, CHRIST!

"I offered my back to those who beat me, my cheeks to those who pulled out my beard; I did not hide my face from mocking and spitting." Isaiah 50:6.

"Prophesy to us, Christ." That was the taunt of the members of the Sanhedrin after convicting Jesus as a blasphemous false prophet worthy of death.

Matthew's gospel says they also "spit in his face and struck him with their fists. Others slapped him" (Matthew 26:67). The Gospel of Mark adds that members of the Sanhedrin blindfolded Jesus, struck him, and then demanded to know "Who hit you?"

Members of the Sanhedrin were infuriated by Jesus' claim that they (the Sanhedrin) would see him "sitting at the right hand of God and coming on the clouds of heaven" (v. 64). If Jesus were that powerful, they reasoned, surely, he would know who hit him, even if he could not see the actions.

One of the great ironies of this story, one scholar noted, is that the eyes of Sanhedrin members were unobstructed, but they were blind to what was happening, while Jesus, with eyes blindfolded, saw exactly what was playing out.

Jesus had gone to Jerusalem with eyes wide open. He knew what to expect. Earlier he had warned the disciples that, "the Son of Man will be betrayed to the chief priests and teachers of the law. They will condemn him to death and will hand him over to the gentiles who will mock him and spit on him, flog him and kill him" (Mark 10:33-34).

Now, as he stood among the Sanhedrin, this prophecy was coming true.

Sanhedrin members might be excused for not knowing about Jesus' recent prophecy. After all, they had not been with Jesus as he traveled from Caesarea Philippi to Jerusalem. But the chief priests and teachers of the law had no reason not to know of another prophecy which their actions helped fulfill that night.

Isaiah 50 is one of a series of Suffering Servant Songs. There is a total of four: Isaiah 42:1-4; Isaiah 49:1-6; Isaiah 50:4-7 and, the most famous, Isaiah 52:13 – 53:12. Each is about Israel's sin, the Suffering Servant's obedience, and the resulting reconciliation made possible. These biblical passages were studied exhaustively by the chief priests and teachers of the law. They were debated passionately.

While each Suffering Servant Song is relevant to this story, consider only verse six of Isaiah 50. There the author wrote of the Suffering Servant, "I offered my back to those who beat me, my cheeks to those who pulled out my beard (some manuscripts say 'slapped'); I did not hide my face from mocking and spitting."

Is that not a clear description of what the members of the Sanhedrin did to Jesus?

Spitting in someone's face was a sign of contempt (Job 30:9-10). It still is. But because the spitting occurred after Jesus' conviction and because it was done by those who judged him guilty, the action showed outrage at what they thought was blasphemy.

Spitting on Jesus was not enough. They beat him, slapped him, and mocked him with shouts of "Prophesy!"

While these religious leaders played a torturous game with Jesus, they unknowingly fulfilled a vital prophecy of their own faith. Each of the offenders probably knew the biblical prophecy by heart since scripture memory was a critical part of their training. Unfortunately, their immediate agenda of convicting a vagabond teacher from Galilee blinded them to what God was doing in their midst.

How ironic that members of the Sanhedrin and the teachers of the law thought themselves on God's side, but their foolish actions made them villains forever.

There were other prophecies going on that night, the prophecies of Judas' betrayal and Peter's denial. Both had been foretold by Jesus and both came painfully true. Later, when Jesus died, another prophecy came true - the destruction of the temple's work. That destruction would be complete three days later when Jesus was raised from the dead just as he had prophesied on the road to Jerusalem when he promised, "Three days later he will rise" (Mark 10:34).

The Son of Man became the Great High Priest who offered himself a once for all sacrifice for the sin of all who would believe. He was the Suffering Servant of Isaiah 50 who took on himself the sins of the world.

At the time, few, if any, recognized all God was about; probably only Jesus, even as he stood among the Sanhedrin with blindfolded eyes. Understanding for others would come, but in time.

How dangerous it is, how foolish it is, how arrogant it is, to conclude, like the Sanhedrin, that our agenda is God's agenda, that our understandings are His. Without compassion and without humility the Sanhedrin screamed, "Prophesy. Tell us who hit you."

Look where the mocking got them.

BOBBY S. (BOB) TERRY

Lord, keep us from prideful and self-serving attitudes about ourselves, about others, and about your will. Amen.

13

FAILURE DOESN'T STOP GOD'S CARING

> "…the rooster crowed. The Lord turned and looked straight at Peter." Luke 22:61

One of the best known "gotcha" moments in the Bible is when the rooster crowed the morning Jesus was crucified. All four gospels – Matthew, Mark, Luke, and John – tell about Peter's bragging the night before. When Jesus told the disciples they would be "scattered like sheep" (Mark 14:27), Peter swore he would follow Jesus, even if it cost him his life.

But before the sun rose the next morning, Peter's courage failed. Around a fire to keep the night chill away, Peter was accused of being a follower of the one on trial for his life about a stone's throw from where Peter stood. Peter's response? "I never knew him," even swearing that he did not know Jesus.

That is when the rooster's cry pierced the night and pierced Peter's soul as well. In various ways, each of the gospels describe Peter's reactions when he realized what he had done – he went out, broke down, and cried bitterly.

BOBBY S. (BOB) TERRY

Luke's gospel relates another part of the story. Luke reports that when the rooster crowed, Jesus turned and looked straight at Peter. Most of us read those words as a "gotcha" moment, an "I told you so" moment, a condemnation for Peter's failure.

But does our concentration on Peter's denial before a hostile crowd cause us to miss part of the story, perhaps an important part?

Luke expands the conversation between Jesus and Peter in which Peter pledged his undying loyalty. The exchange begins with Jesus sharing that Satan asked to "sift Peter." The Bible never defines what "sift" means but from this side of the story, we know Peter was tested like no other follower of Jesus that night.

Jesus did more than share the bad news of what Peter faced. Luke tells us Jesus added, "I have prayed for you." Think of that. Knowing that Peter faced trials, knowing that Peter would deny him, Jesus prayed for Peter. His concern was not anticipating an "I told you so" exchange. Jesus' concern was for Peter and his service in the kingdom.

Jesus added, "When you turn back, strengthen your brothers" (Luke 22:31-32). Denial did not mean that Peter's faith failed. If his faith had failed, Peter's sorrow may have caused him to join Judas at the hanging tree. After all, both denied Jesus that night.

But Jesus said, "I have prayed for you that your faith does not fail." Then he gave him a task. When you have overcome your failure (when you have turned back) strengthen your brothers, Jesus said.

Because we live in a world that relishes "gotcha" movements, we see that message in the locked eyes of Jesus and Peter across the courtyard. "I told you so." That is how we would react.

But what if there were more in the message of that moment? What if Jesus' eyes were filled with compassion? What if his eyes conveyed encouragement, even hope in the midst of such obvious failure? What if Jesus' eyes reminded Peter, "I have prayed for you, so don't give up." What if they said, "Turn back and strengthen your brothers"?

What if we have been wrong all this time and it wasn't a "gotcha" moment at all? Peter still would have wept bitterly at his failure, but the bitterness would be sweetened by the unfailing love of God. Jesus had prayed for him. Jesus still wanted him, still had a task for him.

Wouldn't that message make us cry if we heard it in the midst of our failures?

Mark hints at Jesus' concern for Peter. When the women found an angel at Jesus' empty tomb on resurrection morning, the angel instructed them to "Go tell the disciples and Peter" (Mark 16:7). John's gospel recounts that the first to hear the report of the women were Peter and the disciple whom Jesus loved.

Peter had been sifted by Satan. Peter had failed. But God did not give up on Peter. God still cared for Peter and had work for him to do in the kingdom.

John's gospel closes with another conversation between Jesus and Peter. This time Jesus asked Peter if he loved him. Three times Peter affirmed that he loved Jesus with heart and soul and mind and strength.

Each time Jesus responded with the command, "Feed my sheep." The command was like a sledgehammer pounding a spike. It was clear, certain, and unmistakable. It was like what Jesus said that night in the upper room. "Peter, I have prayed for you. When you turn back, strengthen your brothers."

Peter failed but God did not stop caring about him, did not stop using him in His kingdom. You and I fail, too, but God does not give up on us either. Failure doesn't stop God's caring. God calls us to "turn back" to Him in confession and repentance and then get involved in what He is doing in the world.

Thank you, Lord, for not giving up on us when we fail. Amen.

14

JUDAS AND PETER

"If we confess our sins, he is faithful and just to forgive us our sins and cleanse us from all unrighteousness." I John 1:9

Judas betrayed Jesus. Peter denied Jesus three time. Is one worse than the other?

Judas confessed he had "betrayed innocent blood" and threw the 30 silver coins he was paid for his treachery back at the feet of the chief priests (Matthew 25:3-5). Peter "wept bitterly" when the rooster's crow reminded him of what he had done (Matthew 26:69ff). Even after his eyes fixed on the eyes of Jesus, Peter did not find the courage to confess he really did know the Galilean rabbi.

Judas' guilt drove him to suicide. He hung himself and is universally condemned for his villainy. On that first Easter Sunday morning, Peter gathered with the other disciples (Luke 24:12) and is celebrated as a leader of Christianity.

Both failed that night, but their outcomes are as opposite as opposites can be. Is that fair, some ask? Do the different outcomes say anything about the availability of God's mercy and grace?

Important to the question is the result of the actions of the two disciples. Judas' action resulted in betraying innocent blood. Judas played a key role in turning Jesus over to people plotting to kill him. That was a serious offense. Deuteronomy 27:25 declares, "Cursed be whoever accepts bribes to take the life of innocent blood." Taking innocent blood was considered a pollution (Psalms 106:38-39). It was to be purged from the land (Deuteronomy 21:9).

One scholar wrote taking innocent blood was such a heinous act "that no ordinary repentance affected it."

Judas' actions were intentional and calculated. He took the initiative to seek out the Jewish leaders. He carefully planned how to accomplish the evil deed. He accepted payment for the betrayal.

Some attribute virtuous motives to Judas. Some contend Judas tried to force Jesus to publicly declare himself as Israel's Messiah with signs of power. Some see Jesus' reference to Judas as "friend" (Matthew 26:50) during Jesus' arrest as a sincere description of their relationship rather than a term filled with irony.

But such efforts cannot explain Jesus' words, "Woe to that man who betrays the Son of Man. It would be better for him if he had not been born" (Matthew 26:24). For Jesus, it seems, there was no righteous part of Judas' plan.

Without making excuses for Peter, it should be acknowledged that his denials were impulsive. Earlier that evening he had pledged to follow Jesus even into death (Matthew 26:33). He had defended Jesus with his sword, only to be rebuked by his leader.

When Jesus was led away under arrest, Peter followed, though at some distance. But then his courage failed. His thoughts evidently turned from what was happening to Jesus to what might happen to him. Like that night on the Sea of Galilee (Matthew 14:30), when Peter took his eyes off Jesus, he began to sink. This time he sank deeper and deeper until he swore an oath that he did not know the man.

Peter's actions were about saving his own life. Judas' actions were about taking the life of Jesus.

When Judas recognized his guilt, he went to the chief priests as if seeking absolution. When they could not offer it, he went off by himself and took his own life. There is no indication he attempted to see Jesus (who was on his way to Pilate) or that he sought reconciliation with the disciples. He is pictured alone with the crushing weight of taking innocent blood bearing down.

Peter's recognition of guilt came through a confrontation with Jesus. Luke 22:61 says just as the rooster crowed, "The Lord turned and looked straight at Peter." Peter's bravado about never forsaking Jesus had been as hollow as the smoke from the fire where he warmed himself. Jesus knew it and now Peter did, too.

Peter did not slink off by himself like Judas did. The next time the Bible mentions Peter he is with the disciples on resurrection morning. When Mary announced the Lord had risen, Peter was the first to rush toward the tomb. Perhaps Peter remembered other words of the Lord from their last evening together. After foretelling Peter's denial, Jesus added, "And when you have turned back...." (Luke 22:33). That is what Peter did.

And Judas?

Don't forget that Jesus offered Judas opportunity to repent, as well. Matthew 26 is clear. When Judas asked if he were the one who would betray Jesus, the answer came clearly, "Yes, it is you" (v. 25). The words were tinged with sadness, not bitterness. They dripped with compassion, not anger.

Hours later in the Garden of Gethsemane when Judas led the mob to arrest Jesus, Jesus offered Judas one last chance to turn back from his deadly path. "Judas, are you betraying the Son of Man with a kiss?" (Luke 22:48). Implied was the question, "Judas, are you really going to do this?" Even then the mercy and grace of God was offered the sinner. But Judas would not have it.

The actions of Judas and the actions of Peter are not similar actions. They did not come from similar motivations or have similar results. It is unfair to treat them as if they did. But to both, Jesus offered the mercy and grace of God, even to the last moments. That same mercy and grace is offered to all. Hopefully, we will be like Peter who turned toward Jesus and surrounded himself with fellow believers despite his failure. Hopefully, we will not be like Judas who looked in all the wrong places only to end up alone and on the path toward destruction.

With the Psalmist we pray, "Wash me and I shall be whiter than snow." Amen.

15

ALONE

"Even though I walk through the valley of the shadow of death, I will fear no evil because You are with me."
Psalm 23: 4

The fourth and final Suffering Servant Song in the book of Isaiah paints a tragic and heart-rending picture of the one "who bore the sins of many and made intercession for the transgressor" (Isaiah 53: 12). The complete text is found in Isaiah 52:13 through the end of chapter 53.

The Lord's servant is described as "having no beauty or majesty to attract us to him" in Isaiah 53:2. Verse three adds people "hid their faces from him." No one thought well of the Lord's servant. Instead, they "rejected" him, even "despised" him.

All who saw the Lord's servant, and society in general, concluded God was against this "marred" and "disfigured" human being. They said he was "stricken" by God, "smitten" by God, and even "afflicted" by God (v. 4). How strong the temptation is to see every trouble as evidence of God's displeasure.

GETHSEMANE TO GOLGOTHA

Isaiah describes the Lord's servant as being alone – void of family and friends. He was scorned by individuals and rejected by society. It even appeared God had spurned him.

When the servant was "pierced," no one objected. When he was "crushed," there was no protest. When he was "punished," no one opposed (v. 5). The guilt of others was laid on him and no one challenged the judicial economy (v. 6).

With no human voice of encouragement in his ear, the servant was made a guilt offering for many (v. 10). With no stroke of human compassion on his shoulder, he was "cut off from the land of the living" (v. 8). Through all the suffering of his soul, the servant was alone save for the promise of the third Suffering Servant Song that "He who vindicates me is near" (Isaiah 50:8).

Abandoned. Forsaken. Alone. What a frightening place to be, even for the servant of the Lord.

But that is where Jesus found himself about 700 years after those words were written. Jesus stood with hands bound before the Roman Governor Pilate (Mark 15:1). He had been snatched from private prayer by forces of his own people, his own faith. Now he stood abandoned, forsaken, and alone.

Mark and other gospel writers go to great lengths to remind readers of the parallels between Isaiah's Suffering Servant Songs and the experiences of Jesus.

The previous evening when soldiers came to arrest Jesus, the disciples – his closest followers – fled. They abandoned Jesus just as he had foretold (Mark 14:50). Leading the soldiers was Judas, one of the original 12 disciples (Mark 14:43). Judas had agreed to turn Jesus over to those who wanted him dead. He betrayed Jesus for 30 silver coins. Peter, the leader of the disciples, forsook Jesus. Peter denied even knowing Jesus while Jesus was on trial just steps from where Peter warmed by a fire (Mark 14:72).

The writer of Mark carefully points out others who were against Jesus. Beginning in Mark 14:53, Mark lists the high priests, all the chief priests, elders, teachers of the law, and the whole Sanhedrin. These were the ones "looking for evidence against Jesus so they could put him to death" (v. 55). Mark repeats this list in verse one of the next chapter.

Obviously, the individuals in the group were against Jesus, but the listing shows more. One scholar observed, "The agents who condemned Jesus were not acting as individual groups but as the representative Jewish governing body and as a collective they gave him (Jesus) over to Pilate."

Jesus was alone. His closest followers had abandoned and forsaken him. Jewish leadership unanimously condemned him. Soon the Roman government would find "no fault" in him but still consent to his death.

Crowds of those who cheered him days earlier now despised and rejected him. They thought him a false prophet and hid their faces from him. Jesus was smitten of God, they concluded. He was worthy of the punishment of piercing that came with death on the cross.

Those cheering for his death could not imagine that it was for their transgressions, for their iniquities, for their peace that he endured the suffering of becoming a guilt offering. They could not understand that Jesus, the one foretold in Isaiah as the Lord's servant, "will justify many and he will bear their iniquities" (Isaiah 53:11).

Centuries after the writer of Isaiah affirmed that "He who vindicates me (the Lord's servant) is near," Christians would understand that "God was in Christ reconciling the world to Himself" (2 Corinthians 5:19).

Jesus alone? It certainly appeared so to onlookers. But Jesus was always in the presence of the Father. And so are we when we trust in his sacrificial death as our sin offering.

Lord, help us to know that nothing in all creation shall ever be able to separate us from the Love of God that is Christ Jesus. Amen.

16

HE OPENED NOT HIS MOUTH

"Prophecy never had its origin in the will of man, but men spoke from God as they were carried along by the Holy Spirit." 2 Peter 2: 21

Christians frequently cite the description of God's Suffering Servant described in Isaiah 53 as support for the belief that Jesus was the anointed Suffering Servant foretold by the prophet hundreds of years earlier.

Verse 7 says, in part, the Suffering Servant was "led like a lamb to the slaughter and as a sheep before her shearers is silent, so he did not open his mouth." Christians point to the accounts of the synoptic gospels – Matthew, Mark, and Luke – that when Jesus was on trial for his life, the Roman ruler Pontius Pilate was amazed that Jesus refused to answer a single charge against him.

Matthew 27:13-14 is typical of the reports found in the synoptic gospels. There Matthew writes, "Then Pilate asked him, 'Don't you hear the testimony they are bringing against you?' But Jesus made no reply, not even to a single charge – to the great amazement of the governor."

Matthew and Mark also report that Jesus refused to answer the questions of the Jewish High Priest (Matthew 26:63, Mark 14:61).

Like Isaiah's Suffering Servant, Jesus did not respond to the charges and countercharges of those who sought his life, the Bible says. Before the Jewish High Priest and the Roman Governor, Jesus "did not open his mouth." These reports, Christians generally contend, provide evidence that the death of Jesus fulfilled Isaiah's prophecy and is another validation that Jesus is God's Suffering Servant.

Usually left unnoticed is the conversation between Pilate and Jesus recorded in John's gospel. In John 18:33 – 19:12, Jesus and Pilate have exchanges about Jesus being a king, about the nature of Jesus' kingdom, about the role of Jesus' followers, about truth, and about the source of earthly power.

John even reports exchanges between Jesus and the High Priest in John 18:19-24.

Nowhere in the Bible is there indication of a court record for Jesus' trials. There is nothing to suggest that someone stood nearby writing down every word said. Doubtless, however, some overheard and saw what happened that fateful day. Scholars generally believe their reports must have circulated orally or even in written form as people talked about that day. Early Christians may have been familiar with the reports and made them a resource when the gospels were written thirty or more years later.

More importantly, Jesus promised early believers that the Holy Spirit "will teach you all things and remind you of everything I have said" (John 14:26). In ways no one completely understands, God's Holy Spirit superintended the writing of Scripture.

Perhaps purpose played a role in what each author chose to report. Matthew's gospel, for example, is written to a Jewish audience. Its purpose, scholars agree, is to prove that Jesus was the Jewish Messiah. The gospel of Mark, on the other hand, was likely written at a time early Christians faced persecution. Mark encouraged believers toward discipleship and faithfulness in the face of oppression. Jesus was Exhibit A about being faithful to God.

The exact date and the exact order in which the gospels were written is uncertain. It is generally believed that Matthew, Mark, and Luke were all written in the 50s or 60s, certainly before the destruction of Jerusalem in 70 AD.

John was probably written in the 90s AD. By that time, the church faced a new problem. Increasingly, the church was shedding its Jewish roots as the faith took hold across Europe and North Africa. There are even reports of missionary activity as far away as India by this time. Was the church a new political movement that threatened the Roman Empire?

Christians understood their kingdom – the Kingdom of God – transcended earthly kingdoms. They were not about military power or the power to rule. But they were about truth, a truth to which even Roman authority (and civil authority for all time) would be accountable.

From resources available to him, and under the superintendence of the Holy Spirit, John affirmed these truths in the exchanges between Jesus and Pilate. In a series of questions and responses, Jesus affirms to Pilate that he (Jesus) is a king, but his kingdom is not "of this world." That is why Jesus' followers did not rise up to defend him. For readers of John's gospel, the church was not a threat to Rome.

But the church proclaimed the truth. That truth was that Jesus was the eternal king - the king who could forgive sin, conquer death, and give eternal life. Pilate and every Roman official, like all people everywhere, would be held accountable for their responses to that truth.

For the purposes of Matthew, Mark, and Luke it was important to emphasize that Jesus was like a lamb "who opened not his mouth." Nothing in John suggests that Jesus responded in any other way than a "lamb who was silent" to any of the criminal charges or political maneuverings of the Jewish leaders as he stood before Pilate. That description is still appropriate.

John adds that Jesus bore witness before Pilate to the truth to which all people everywhere will be held accountable. "Everyone on the side of truth listens to me," said Jesus (John 18:37). And Jesus earlier said, "I am the way, the truth, and the life, and no man comes to the Father except by me" (John 14:6). Readers of John's gospel recognized that teaching, also.

Knowing the purposes of the gospel writers, the time of writings, and the life situations of the writings may help one better understand the writings themselves and how all Scripture fits together.

Father, help us to study your Word as workmen who need not be ashamed. Amen.

17

TO PLEASE THE CROWD

"He (Pilate) had Jesus flogged and handed him over to be crucified."
Mark 15:15.

What crime did Jesus commit that made him worthy of death? The Jews called him a blasphemer and worthy of death. But the determination of whether Jesus would live or die was made by the Roman governor Pontius Pilate. What Roman law had Jesus broken that permitted Pilate to sentence him to death?

Some scholars argue that Jesus broke a political law; that he claimed to be king of the Jews. Tiberius was Emperor of Rome at the time and he would tolerate no other king. When Jesus was called king of the Jews, that made him an enemy of Rome, which always resulted in the death penalty, these academics argue.

In Mark 15:9 and 12, Pilate twice identifies Jesus as king of the Jews. Some reason Pilate had already found Jesus guilty but was willing to release him as part of upholding the tradition of annually releasing a prisoner during the Passover celebration.

That conclusion is suspect because two verses later Pilate asks the crowd, "What crime has he done?" On its face, it seems Mark presents Pilate as also seeking an answer about what Roman law Jesus broke that justified his crucifixion.

John's gospel provides additional insight. Three times Pilate tells the Jews, "I find no basis for a charge against this man" (John 18:38, 19:4, 6).

Luke's gospel is equally clear. Three times (Luke 23:4, 14, 22) Pilate says, "I find no basis for a charge against this man."

Even to a casual reader these accounts, taken together, appear to confirm that Jesus had violated no Roman law, let alone a law worthy of the death penalty.

Unfortunately, a Jew did not have to break a Roman law in order to suffer death at the hands of Romans at this time in history. Roman citizens were protected from arbitrary abuse. In Acts 22, the Apostle Paul recounts getting out of a beating because he was a Roman citizen.

But judicial procedures for dealing with one who was not a Roman citizen in a distant and insignificant place like Judea were not clearly outlined, historians say. Would Tiberius Caesar care if Pilate had a wandering rabbi crucified? Would the emperor be concerned if Pilate released a popular Jewish figure who claimed to be king of the Jews?

Basically, Pilate held the fate of Jesus in his own hands. Pilate could do whatever he decided to do.

John 19 describes how the Jews tried to play the political card. They threatened Pilate, saying words to the effect that if you release someone who claims to be a king, you are no friend of Caesar (Tiberius).

Three of the gospels (Matthew, Luke, and John) indicate Pilate argued with Jewish leaders and then the Jewish crowd about Jesus' punishment. Finally, Pilate gave up and gave in. John says, "Finally Pilate handed him over" (John 19:16). Luke says, "Pilate decided to grant their demand" (Luke 23:24). Matthew writes, "He (Pilate) had Jesus flogged and handed him over to them" (Matthew 27:26).

Mark provides an additional insight. Mark says Pilate gave Jesus over to be crucified because he "wanted to please the crowd" (Mark 15:15).

Pilate's primary concern, according to Mark, was not about Roman law. It was not about what was right or true. It was not about others or even the welfare of the society he governed. All of these bowed to Pilate's primary motivation – self.

John hints that the political card played by the Jews threatened the Judean governor. Mark lays it out plainly. Pilate willingly sacrificed the life of Jesus in order to curry favor with the crowd. Everything else paled before Pilate's personal desire.

Pilate's protestations of his innocence related to Jesus' death (washing his hands of Jesus' blood) were only that, hollow protestations. Pilate chose self-interest. He wanted to please the crowd even when he knew the crowd was wrong.

Jesus broke no Roman law. He committed no crime. But none of that mattered when truth ran up against self-interest.

Like Pilate, we face times when we feel threatened, times when we want to "please the crowd." What are we willing to sacrifice at such times? Are we guided by moral commitments to truth, to others, to God? Or are our choices motivated by self-interest?

Just how much like Pilate are we?

Lord, help us live in truth with one another and before You. Amen.

18

JEALOUSY AND ZEAL

> "He knew it was out of envy that they had handed Jesus over to him." Matthew 27:18

Pilate was a savvy politician. He had to be to rise from the Equestrian class of Roman citizens to be appointed by the emperor as governor of Judea, an assignment that included Samaria and Idumea as well. Evidently, he was shrewd, at least shrewd enough to hold onto that job for a decade while various political currents swept over the Roman Empire.

The Bible indicates Pilate was also perceptive. The gospels of Matthew and Mark both indicate Pilate knew the trial of Jesus was a setup. He understood the Jewish leaders were jealous of Jesus' influence among the Jewish people; that it was envy that caused the chief priests, elders, and teachers of the law to turn Jesus over to him for trial (Matthew 27:18, Mark 15:10).

Unfortunately, translating the Greek word used by the gospel writers as envy or jealousy fails to capture all the writers may have intended.

The Greek word is phthonos. It describes an array of emotions expressing violent dislike of something. In the story of Daniel, the word is used to describe the feelings of the Persian satraps toward Daniel. The phthonos of the satraps caused Daniel to be thrown into the lion's den.

The word carries other implications. Scholars point out the kind of envy or jealousy described relates closely to zeal. Not only were the satraps jealous of Daniel, they were zealous for their own ways. Some interbiblical period writings actually equate phthonos (jealous) with zelos (zeal) (1 Maccabees 8:16). In Hebrew, the word for "jealous of" can also be translated "zealous for," scholars say. The root word of both is the same.

A perceptive Pilate may have understood that Jewish leaders were jealous of Jesus and that their jealousy was based in their zeal for Jewish law and for the temple. Jesus did not understand the law as the Jewish leaders did. He healed on the Sabbath. He flaunted certain food laws. More importantly, Jesus threatened the temple, they believed.

Remember, Jesus' words about destroying the temple played a key role in the deliberations before the Sanhedrin.

Pilate was well acquainted with Jewish zeal. History teaches that most of his conflict with Jewish leaders related to their intransigent devotion to Jewish law. It is no stretch of the imagination to think that a savvy, shrewd, and perceptive politician understood that zeal for their law fueled the envy and jealousy toward Jesus so publicly displayed that tragic day.

The Apostle Paul's persecution of the early church illustrates the fuller meaning of phthonos. It was his zeal for the law and his jealousy of the spread of Christian faith that convinced him that he "ought to do all that is possible to oppose the name of Jesus of Nazareth" (Acts 26:9). It is as if the two fed on one another. Zeal fired jealousy and jealousy stimulated zeal.

The result was a "win-at-all-cost" attitude. Daniel could be thrown to the lions. Jesus could be crucified. Paul could drag Christians from synagogue to prison with no remorse. The ends justified the means. All else could be sacrificed in order to win.

Paul's letters indicate this attitude sometimes impacted the early church. In Philippians 1:15ff, Paul writes, "It is true that some preach Christ out of envy and rivalry" (phthonos). He says they preach out of selfish ambition and try to cause Paul trouble while he is in chains. In his first letter to Timothy, Paul cautions about people whose work results in "envy, strife, malicious talk, evil suspicions, constant friction," and more (1 Timothy 6:4-5).

Sadly, there is indication that the spirit of phthonos may have played a role in the martyrdom of both Peter and Paul. A first-century writing known as 1 Clement says, "Through jealousy and phthonos the greatest and most righteous pillars (of the church) were persecuted and their death desired." The writing comes from Rome and was addressed to the church at Corinth. The reference, scholars believe, is to the deaths of Peter and Paul.

Jealousy and zeal can be a deadly combination. Pilate recognized that "win-at-all-cost" attitude among those who accused Jesus. Clement says it played a part in the deaths of Peter and Paul. How many others in Christian history and in today's church have been wounded or killed by a phthonos-like attitude?

A "win-at-all-cost" attitude is about me and mine. It is about my party, about my way. It has little to do with the gospel.

Lord, in our devotion to You, may we be guided by Your voice and not our own echoes. Amen.

19

WHO YOU BELIEVE IS IMPORTANT

"As soon as the chief priests and their officials saw him (Jesus), they shouted, 'Crucify! Crucify!'" John 19:6

For centuries, readers of the Bible have scratched their heads in bewilderment about how the Passover crowd in Jerusalem could turn on Jesus so quickly. On Sunday of that fateful week, the people cheered Jesus as coming Messiah. On Friday, they screamed for Jesus to be crucified. How could that happen?

All the gospels affirm that Jesus' popularity carried over well into the week. Luke makes it the clearest. In Luke 19:48, after Jesus' Triumphal Entry, the writer says, "all the people hung on his words." In the next chapter, one reads, "…while all the people were listening, Jesus said…" (Luke 20:45). Luke 21:38 declares, "All the people came early to hear him in the temple."

Day after day the people crowded around Jesus as he taught in the temple. He was so popular it scared the chief priests and other authorities. Three times Luke says the chief priests and teachers of the law wanted to do Jesus harm but were stopped by fear of the people (Luke 19:47, 20:19, 22:2).

On Friday morning all that changed. By nine o'clock Jesus stood bound like a criminal before Pilate, the Roman ruler. He looked battered from where he had been beaten, slapped, and portions of his beard pulled out. Mark 15:3 says, "The chief priests accused him of many things." In John 18:30, the Jewish leaders called Jesus a criminal.

Yet, Pilate, after examining Jesus, announced, "I find no basis for a charge against him" (John 18:38).

To the Jewish onlooker, perhaps a religious pilgrim come to Jerusalem to celebrate the Passover, this was a strange scene. Jewish leaders accused a fellow Jew and the Roman governor defended him. Usually, it was the Romans - the foreigners, the invaders, the conquerors, the occupiers, the infidels – who accused and abused the Jews. Usually, it was the Jewish leaders who attempted to mediate circumstances to save one of their own.

Pilate heard the priests say that Jesus was from Galilee. He concluded that might be his way out of the dilemma between his own moral code and the public pressure he faced from the Jews. Pilate ruled Samaria, Judea, and Idumea. Galilee was governed by Herod Antipas and had been for nearly 30 years. They were like separate states. Pilate tried to make Jesus Herod's problem, not his. He sent Jesus to Herod who was in Jerusalem for the Passover (Luke 23:6ff). Herod talked to Jesus but sent him back to Pilate with an indication of innocence.

By late morning Jesus once again stood before Pilate. The gospel writers seem to stress that Pilate wanted to let Jesus go. Matthew's gospel says Pilate knew the Jewish leaders envied Jesus (Matthew 23:18). The writer goes so far as to say Pilate knew Jesus was innocent (v. 23). The Gospel of John repeatedly quotes Pilate saying, "I find no basis for a charge against him" (18:38, 19:4, 19:6).

The Jewish leaders would have none of it. They worked the crowd to demand death for Jesus. Mark 15:11 says, "But the chief priests stirred up the crowd." Matthew 23:20 says the chief priests and elders persuaded the crowd.

The crowd, the people – those who hailed Jesus King and Messiah on Sunday. Those who hung on his every word on Monday. Those who came early to get a good seat to hear Jesus on Tuesday and Wednesday. To these, the chief priests, elders, and scribes said Jesus was worthy of death. They label him a false prophet and a threat to the nation. They called him a troublemaker and a lawbreaker.

Their words were vehement (Luke 23:10) leaving no doubt about the outcome the Jewish authorities sought. Jesus was guilty. Jesus should die and Jesus should die that day. One who violated the Law of Moses was to die without mercy (Deuteronomy 17: 6-7).

Yet, Pilate stood before the Passover crowd and said he found no reason that Jesus should die. He added that Herod Antipas also examined Jesus and found nothing about him deserving death.

Who would the crowd – the people - believe? Would they believe their chief priests, their elders, their teachers of the law, and members of the Sanhedrin? Or would they believe the Roman ruler or Herod Antipas? The Jews never liked the Herod family – not the father when he ruled and not the sons now. The Herods were no better than the Romans to most Jews.

Pilate tried one more time to free Jesus. He appealed to the custom of Rome releasing one Jewish prisoner as a sign of goodwill on the feast of Passover. He suggested Jesus but the chief priests and teachers of the law asked for Barabbas – a man who had committed murder during recent riots in Jerusalem. Their concern was not about Barabbas' freedom. It was about Jesus' death.

The people's choice was made. The cry "Barabbas" grew until it echoed off the foundation of Temple Mount and off the rocks of the adjacent Antonio Fortress, Rome's stronghold in the city. It was a full-throated cry from an enraged crowd, a bloodlust cry. The people chose to believe the chief priests. They chose to believe Jesus an imposter. They concluded he should be cursed by hanging on a tree in death. He was not Messiah. He was not even a true prophet.

When Pilate yielded to the power of what had turned into a mob, the crowd cried, "His blood on us and on our children." What a tragedy of history those words.

One can only wonder what members of the crowd thought about their actions the day after Jesus died. Or what they thought when word spread that Jesus had been raised from the dead. One can only speculate about what members of the crowd felt when the Apostle Peter stood at Pentecost and declared, "You, with wicked men, put him to death by nailing him to the cross" (Acts 2:23).

The crowd believed the lies of their leaders. They rejected the truth because it came from those considered enemies. They people acted on untruth and are forever associated with the villainy of their decision.

Who the people chose to believe made a difference that day. Who one chooses to believe makes a difference today, too.

Lord, help us not to put our faith in any human being but only in You. Amen

20

WEIGHED AND FOUND WANTING

> "When Jesus said this, one of the officials nearby struck him in the face. 'Is this the way you answer the high priest?' he demanded."
> John 18: 22

Following Jesus' arrest, the Gospel of John says Jesus was taken first to Annas. Although Annas was not the High Priest, he was a powerful figure. He had been appointed High Priest by Quirinius when he was governor of Syria in 6 AD and served for 9 years. And in the 50 years after his removal, five of his sons, his son-in law, and grandson all became High Priest. Annas was the proverbial power behind the throne, even for Caiaphas, his son-in-law who was High Priest at the time.

Before the High Priest, even a former High Priest, one was expected to be humble, meek, and subservient. Not Jesus. Most scholars and historians speak of Jesus being on trial before Annas. In truth, it was the other way around. Annas, the patriarch of high priests, was on trial before Jesus. At this late moment would Annas see the truth? Would he listen to Jesus? Would he side with truth?

John's description of Jesus' time before Annas indicates the former High Priest never intended to seek truth. He only sought evidence to support the death sentence for Jesus that had already been determined. Jewish law specifies one may not testify against himself. Yet, Annas questioned Jesus about his teachings.

When Jesus told him he should ask those who listened to his teaching instead of harassing him, a temple policeman struck Jesus for insubordination. The blow was more than a slap. It was a decisive rejection of the truth by Annas as well as the policeman.

Annas, powerful, proud, and arrogant, was tried and found wanting because he would not see and believe the truth about Jesus.

Caiaphas and members of the Sanhedrin also refused to see who Jesus was. Mark 14:53-65 recounts Jesus preaching the truth to them about who he was – "the Christ, the Son of the Blessed One." But instead of believing, they found Jesus worthy of death.

Their failure to believe the message directly from the mouth of Jesus showed they had been weighed and found wanting.

Herod Antipas was just as blind. He had ruled Galilee since the death of his father Herod the Great and the fame of Jesus had not escaped him. But Herod Antipas only saw Jesus as some kind of magician able to do miraculous tricks.

When Jesus refused to respond to his endless questions, Herod dismissed him as unworthy of his attention, let alone his devotion.

Pilate was equally confused. He claimed to hold life and death power over Jesus, but Jesus responded that the only power Pilate had was the power allowed by God (John 19:10-11). Pilate asked serious questions. Perhaps he tried to understand. But in the end, he, too, chose not to believe the truth, not to listen to Jesus. Instead, Pilate sent Jesus to his death. It was pure mockery when Pilate had a sign nailed to Jesus' cross proclaiming him King of the Jews.

When Pilate stood before Jesus, he sided with error over truth. He, too, was weighed and found wanting.

Hours later, with life almost gone, Jesus declared, "It is finished" and "gave up his spirit." The price of sin's forgiveness was paid. Jesus became "a ransom for many."

Why did he choose such a path? Jesus answered that question when he said, "For God so loved the world that he gave his one and only son that whoever believes in him should not perish but have everlasting life" (John 3:16).

He did it so people like Annas, Caiaphas, Herod Antipas, Pilate, you, and me might have opportunity to hear and believe in Jesus, "the Lamb of God who takes away the sins of the world."

Lord, help us to respond positively when you speak to our hearts. Amen.

21

UNLIKELY COMPANIONS

"I have sinned for I have betrayed innocent blood." Matthew 27:4

Matthew's gospel describes two characters in the passion of our Lord who appear trapped and unable (or unwilling) to get out of the systems that bound them. Neither seemed to realize that failing to make a decision, failing to take decisive action to change one's conditions, is the same as making a decision. Failing to act is a decision to be carried along by circumstances rather than trying to influence what goes on around you.

As unlikely as it seems, Judas, a disciple of Jesus, and Pilate, the Roman governor, have a number of similarities as Matthew tells their stories in chapter 27.

Judas and Pilate enter the passion story at different places. Judas initiates the tragic account when he guides an armed crowd to arrest Jesus. Judas betrays Jesus. He turns Jesus over to the Jewish crowd that plotted ways to take his life.

Pilate enters when the Jewish High Priest and others bring the bound and beaten Jesus to be tried by the Roman governor. It would not be long before Pilate, too, turned Jesus over to the crowd. Pilate was supposed to govern Judea according to Roman law, but not this time.

Why Judas did what he did is never explained. The most offered explanation is greed. And why Pilate yielded to pressure rather than upholding the law can only be explained by expediency. Both have their roots in concern for self.

The decisions by the Jewish disciple and the Roman ruler both resulted in personal feelings of guilt. That is what happens when one deliberately chooses to violate the ethical and moral standards by which one lives or of the community of which one is a part.

To ease his guilt, Judas tried to get out of the bargain made with the chief priests. He went back to the temple and confessed he had "betrayed innocent blood" (v. 4). Not long afterwards Pilate rejected any responsibility for what was about to happen to Jesus. "I am innocent of this man's blood," he told the crowd (v. 24). Judas knew he was responsible. Pilate never acknowledged his role.

Words about personal guilt and responsibility were not enough for either Judas or Pilate. Both dramatized their feelings with actions. Judas acted out his anguish by throwing the 30 silver coins he received for betraying Jesus into the temple where the chief priests stood (v. 5). Evidently, the money had come from the temple treasury in the first place. Now Judas tried to give it back.

Pilate ordered a bowl of water brought to him. Before the crowd, he washed his hands symbolizing he bore no guilt for allowing Jesus to be killed.

Pilate said he "found no fault" in Jesus but still consented to his death. No wonder Pilate had guilt issues.

"It is your responsibility," Pilate declared to the crowd (v. 24). Ironically, those are the same words the chief priests said to Judas, "It is your responsibility" (v. 4). Pilate said the words to others – the crowd. Judas heard the words from others – the chief priests. But were they really in different places? At different points in the process, both turned Jesus over to be crucified. Each carried the weight of that decision.

When Judas returned the 30 pieces of silver to the chief priests, the coins could not be put back into the temple treasury. The priests called the money "blood money" (v. 6). They decided to buy a plot of land where strangers who died in Jerusalem could be buried. One author points out that to be considered "blood money" the chief priests had to know the money was used against an innocent person. Otherwise, the money could be returned to the treasury. If so, even that small detail provides insight into the shared responsibility of others for the shed blood of Jesus.

There is another similarity. Neither Judas nor Pilate had the courage to stop what was about to happen. Judas had opportunity to turn away from his agreement to betray Jesus. He could have confessed and repented in the upper room when Jesus confronted him with his treachery. He could have refused to lead the crowd to the place where Jesus prayed. He could have refused to identify Jesus. He did none of these. Once events were in motion, Judas took the easy way out and let events play out as they would.

Pilate had opportunity to stop what was about to happen, but he did not. Even though he found no fault in him, Pilate betrayed Jesus into the hands of the blood-thirsty crowd. He allowed events to play out rather than taking a stand.

Judas and Pilate, unlikely companions. Both caught up in circumstances. Both unwilling to make a difference. How tragic.

Father, help us always choose to do what is right rather than be carried along by circumstances. Amen.

22

A BRIEF ENCOUNTER – SIMON

> "A certain man from Cyrene, Simon, the father of Alexander and Rufus, was passing by on his way in from the country and they forced him to carry the cross." Mark 15:21

Jesus had been beaten, flogged, and mocked by the Roman soldiers. He had been sentenced to death by Pilate and turned over to the soldiers who led him out for crucifixion. What happened next provides insight into how cruelly Jesus had been treated by the Romans. The writers of the gospels of Matthew, Mark, and Luke each tell the story of the guards seizing a passerby and forcing him to carry Jesus' cross.

Roman practice required the condemned to carry his cross (at least the crossbeam of the cross) from the place where he was condemned to the site of execution. Usually, the cross was placed on the back of the neck like a yoke and the condemned carried it by wrapping his arms around both ends of the crossbeam.

Evidently, Jesus had been so badly beaten he was unable to carry the cross. He needed help in order to live long enough for the death sentence to be carried out. Some scholars point to this incident as partial explanation of why Jesus died so quickly once he was nailed to the cross.

The three synoptic gospels all agree the person forced to carry Jesus' cross was Simon from Cyrene. Scholars disagree about whether he was a Jew or gentile. About 300 years earlier, a group of Jews had been forcibly resettled in Cyrenaica (what is now eastern Libya) and Cyrene was its capital city. That Jews from there regularly traveled back to Jerusalem is attested to in Acts 6:9, which describes a Jerusalem synagogue that served Jews from Cyrenaica.

At the same time, the name Simon was considered a Greek name, even though it was often substituted for the Hebrew name Simeon. The Gospel of Mark adds that Simon was the father of Rufus and Alexander. Since neither of those names is considered a Hebrew name, some believe Simon was a gentile.

Either way, Simon was headed into Jerusalem from the countryside when the Roman soldiers commandeered him and forced him to carry Jesus' cross. If he were a religious pilgrim or if he were returning to the city from some errand, being forced by Roman soldiers to carry an instrument of execution must have been a frightening experience. Usually, the person carrying the crossbeam was the individual crucified.

First century Gnostics seized on this incident and offered a novel explanation for their view of the crucifixion. Generally, Gnostics believed that flesh (the material world) was evil and knowledge was good. Jesus, they said, only "appeared" in human form but his "reality" was knowledge. Since knowledge could not be crucified, Gnostics taught that Simon was the one actually nailed to the cross while Jesus stood by and watched.

Islam embraces a somewhat similar view based on this story. Islam teaches that Simon and not Jesus was crucified because he was the one who carried the crossbeam to Golgotha.

Early Christians condemned such views as heresy. Simon carried the crossbeam, as the Bible says, but the flesh and blood Jesus was the one crucified, the church taught. In addition, many believed that Simon not only carried the cross but that he became one of the eyewitnesses who testified that Jesus really was crucified.

Matthew, Mark, and Luke all give Simon's name as the one coerced into carrying the cross. They do not say some anonymous passerby was forced to do so. Evidently, the gospel writers expected their readers to be familiar with his name. Mark goes even farther. In Mark 15:21, the writer says this Simon is the father of Rufus and Alexander. The only explanation for including such otherwise throwaway information is that Mark expected his readers to know the sons as well as the father. And, if the early Christian community did not know Simon, how did any of the gospel writers know who this unfortunate passerby was in the first place, let alone know the name of his sons, more than a decade after the actual event?

Nothing in the Bible indicates that Simon had any kind of relationship with Jesus before he was shanghaied to carry Jesus' cross. However, there is every reason to believe that like the thief who asked Jesus to remember him when Jesus came into his kingdom, and like the Roman centurion who confessed Jesus as the son of God, Simon's brief encounter with Jesus was enough to change his life.

Many believe Simon became a follower of Jesus, a verifier of the crucifixion, and a witness to his own community. Some believe he eventually served as a bishop before being martyred in 100 AD. December 1 is even a feast day for Simon in some Christian traditions.

Certainly, Christian believers from Cyrene soon became prominent in the missionary work of the church. After the persecution of Jesus-followers in Jerusalem following the martyrdom of Stephen, Acts 11:21-22 reports men from Cyrene went to Antioch and shared the gospel with the Greeks. "The Lord's hand was with them, and a great number of people believed and turned to the Lord," the verse says.

In Acts 13:1, Lucius of Cyrene is listed as a "prophet and teacher" in the Antioch church.

This understanding of scripture may be the most reasonable explanation of why the name of the one who carried Jesus' cross to Golgotha was important enough to be remembered. It explains why Simon's name was important enough to be written down in three of the gospels and why Mark included the name of Simon's sons. It also provides a direct link to why the distant Cyrenaic community so quickly played a major role in the spread of the gospel.

One thing is sure. A brief encounter with Jesus can change a life forever. It did for the thief of the cross. It did for the centurion. Christian tradition says it did for Simon of Cyrene. It did for me, and it can for you.

Lord, thank you for breaking into our lives that we might believe. Amen.

23

THEY OFFERED HIM WINE

"They offered him a wine vinegar." Luke 23:36

Each of the four gospels tells the story of Jesus being offered wine. But each of the stories is a little different from the others. For example, Matthew and Mark tell of Jesus being offered wine two different times. Luke and John each recount only one time. And while Matthew and Mark relate similar accounts of Jesus being offered wine, they disagree on the kind of wine he was offered.

In Mark 15:23, we are told Jesus was first offered "wine mixed with myrrh." That made it a fragrant, sweet tasting wine. Matthew, on the other hand, says the first wine offered was mixed with gall (Matthew 27:34) which made it bitter. Interestingly, both gospels hint that the first drink was offered to Jesus before the actual crucifixion. Matthew lays out the events as: 1. arriving at Golgotha; 2. offering Jesus wine; 3. the actual crucifixion. Mark offers a similar pattern of events in Mark 15:22-24.

The single offering of wine in Luke and John clearly occurred after Jesus was nailed to the cross.

Offering wine to the condemned was a common practice in New Testament times. Jewish writings tell of a group of Jerusalem women who gave scented wine to the condemned as an act of piety. It was thought scented wine numbed the victims and lessen their suffering. One Talmudic source even instructs, "The condemned... are given to drink wine containing (spices) so that they should not feel grieved."

Tertullian, an early church father, relates the story of a Christian catechumen who had been condemned to death being given "medicated wine" by friends as an analgesic to the pain he faced.

The practice should not be surprising since Proverbs 31:6 counsels, "Give strong drink to the one who is ready to perish...."

Mark uses the Greek word oinos to describe the sweet wine mixed with myrrh first offered to Jesus. Scholars say that would be consistent with local practices, as would offering the wine before the actual crucifixion.

But Jesus refused the wine according to both Mark and Matthew. Bible students have long pondered why Jesus refused Mark's sweet wine that would have eased his suffering on the cross. Some point back to the Last Supper where Jesus said he would not drink again until "I drink again in the kingdom of God" (Mark 14:25). Refusing the sweet wine, these contend, was keeping that promise.

Others ask if Jesus' comment made around the table referenced a simple drink to ease thirst or was it more akin to participating in a banquet meal. They point to John's account of Jesus being offered wine where the writer says Jesus was offered and received the wine to drink (John 19:29-30).

Jesus' refusal of the sweet wine may be Mark's way of focusing attention on Jesus' commitment to his redemptive purpose. In the Garden of Gethsemane, Jesus submitted completely to the "cup" of suffering death. He would have to drink the last bitter dregs. A medicated wine that numbed his senses would be at cross-purposes with that goal.

Jesus may have viewed the wine mixed with myrrh as another temptation. To drink it would be like breaking his promise. Instead, Jesus chose to give himself fully and completely to his redemptive task including all its physical pain and suffering.

Matthew uses the Greek word oxos to describe the wine first offered to Jesus. It is a wine mixed with gall, a bitter wine. One can almost see Jesus spitting it out of his mouth because it tasted so bad. Matthew's account is more polite. The writer says, "After tasting it, Jesus refused to drink it" (Matthew 27:34). Mark has Jesus refusing something physically desirable. Matthew describes Jesus refusing something hard to swallow.

Instead of directing attention to the total self-giving of Jesus, Matthew may be pointing readers to another way the offering of wine fulfilled prophesy related to the Messiah.

Psalms 69:21 reads, "They put gall in my food and gave me vinegar for my thirst." The church has long looked at this psalm of David as pointing toward Christ, much like Psalm 22 does. Verse four of Psalm 69 references the unjust opposition to Jesus, and verse nine emphasizes Jesus' passion for the kingdom of God. Early Christians saw verse 21 as pointing to the cross and the offering of wine to the condemned.

Matthew and Mark both report the second wine offered Jesus was wine vinegar. Luke and John say wine vinegar was offered in their single accounts. All four writers point back to Psalm 69:21. John goes so far as to specify that wine vinegar was given Jesus in response to his cry, "I am thirsty" (John 19:29). Each one would be partial fulfillment of the prophecy.

But Matthew drives the point home with complete fulfillment of the prophecy. Gall and vinegar were both offered Jesus during his crucifixion. Gall was part of the first wine offering while vinegar was the second, just as Psalm 69:21 declared.

Mark may want readers to see the total self-giving of Jesus as the Lamb of God that takes away the sins of the world. And Matthew may want readers to recognize that all of this was part of God's plan to rescue lost humanity.

Lord, thank you that before the foundation of the world, you chose to save us through the sacrifice of your Son, our Savior. Amen.

24

THEY DO NOT KNOW

"Father, forgive them for they do not know what they are doing."
Luke 23:34

It may seem odd that Jesus prayed for those responsible for taking his life, even while he hung on a cross. One might expect to hear cries for revenge or worse. But Jesus prayed, "Father, forgive them for they do not know what they are doing" (Luke 23:34). On reflection, however, it becomes clear that this prayer from the cross embodied the tone of Jesus' ministry from its earliest days. And it is still supposed to characterize the lives of Christians.

In the Sermon on the Mount, Jesus taught his followers to "love your enemies and pray for those who persecute you" (Matthew 5:44). The Gospel of Luke expands Jesus' instructions related to loving one's enemies. There Jesus urged, "Love your enemies, do good to those who hate you. Bless those who curse you and pray for those who mistreat you" (Luke 6:27-28).

What Jesus taught, he practiced. Both Matthew and Luke record Jesus praying for Jerusalem even though it was the city that killed the prophets and rejected God's messengers (Matthew 23:37, Luke

13:34). Luke says Jesus prayed for the city just after acknowledging that he had to hurry there "because no prophet can die outside of Jerusalem."

Odd, too, is the reason Jesus asked God to forgive those who conspired to take his life, along with those who abused and tortured him. Jesus sought God's forgiveness of them because "they do not know what they are doing."

Even to the casual reader it is clear the Romans knew what they were doing. The soldiers tortured Jesus as an upstart political prisoner who dared claim he was a king. The Romans intended to show everyone what happened to people who challenged the primacy of Caesar. Equally clear is the motivation of the Jewish rulers, elders, and chief priests. They were ridding themselves of another messianic pretender before he upset the delicate political balance between the Jews and the Romans.

So how does one understand Jesus' words, "They do not know what they are doing"?

The Apostle Paul's testimony provides a helpful insight. As he stood before King Herod Agrippa, Paul confessed, "I, too, was convinced that I ought to do all that was possible to oppose the name of Jesus of Nazareth" (Acts 26:9). After describing ways he persecuted Christians out of a zeal for God, according to the Jewish law, Paul told Agrippa his story of meeting the Lord and how his life was changed. When Paul met Jesus, he came to understand that he had not known what he was doing when he persecuted early Christians.

The Apostle Peter made a similar point in his sermon to the people of Jerusalem recorded in Acts 3:11 ff. After recounting how they had crucified Jesus, Peter said, "Now brothers, I know that you acted in ignorance as did your leaders" (v. 17).

Evidently, both Peter and Paul believed those responsible for Jesus' death – Jew and Roman - did not understand what God was doing in Jesus. They were like those referred to by Jesus in Mark 4:12

when he quoted from Isaiah about those who are "ever seeing but never perceiving" or "ever hearing but never understanding."

If those who crucified Jesus had perceived or understood, they would not have opposed God's representative. Peter hinted at this in verse 18 when he added, "But this is how God fulfilled what he had foretold through the prophets saying that his Christ would suffer."

Caiaphas, the Jewish High Priest, acted purposefully against Jesus. But Jesus' prayer indicates Caiaphas did not know what he was doing. The Sanhedrin took deliberate steps to have Jesus crucified but, according to Jesus, they did not know what they were doing. Pilate acted high-handedly in forfeiting Jesus' life but he, too, did not understand. Even those in the crowd who enthusiastically taunted Jesus in his final hours, did not know what they were doing.

Sometimes it is hard to believe that deliberate, purposeful, high-handed, enthusiastic acts of enemies can be based on ignorance. Yet, that is exactly what Jesus said. That is what Peter and Paul wrote. And that is what the early church practiced.

A few years after Jesus' death and resurrection, Stephen, a deacon and evangelist, lay crumpled on the ground from the stones beating him to death. There he prayed, "Lord, do not lay this sin against them" (Acts 7:60). In about 60 A.D., the Jewish High Priest Annas II had James, the half-brother of Jesus, stoned. Christian tradition teaches that James knelt and prayed the words of Jesus, "Father forgive them for they do not know what they are doing" as he died.

Ignatius, bishop of Antioch, who died about 108 A.D., urged early Christians, many of them facing martyrdom, to "offer prayers in response to their blasphemies…be gentle in response to their cruelty and do not be eager to imitate them in return…Let us eagerly be imitators of the Lord."

That was a difficult example to follow then, and it is a difficult example to follow now. Yet, it is important to remember that Jesus taught even when opposition and persecution is purposeful, deliberate, high-handed, and enthusiastic, its advocates still may not know what they are doing. That is why early Christians lived and died with mercy and grace, just as Jesus did. Today's Christians can do no less.

Lord, give us strength to repay evil with blessings just as you did on the cross. Amen.

25

TWO THIEVES

"And he was numbered with the transgressors." Isaiah 53:12

Every year, millions of Christians from around the world travel to Jerusalem to retrace the steps of Jesus by walking the Way of the Cross. That is the name given to the route Jesus supposedly took as he made his way from the place of judgment to the place of execution. At each station of the cross, a picture is engraved into a nearby stone building depicting what took place on that spot.

Interestingly, none of the pictures indicate that Jesus was accompanied by other prisoners marching to their death. Most Christians think of Jesus making the journey accompanied only by Roman soldiers and a passerby named Simon who was forced to carry Jesus' cross.

However, the Gospel of Luke says differently. Luke is the only place in the Bible that reports, "Two other men, both criminals, were also led out with him to be executed" (Luke 23:32). Whether Jesus led the parade of the condemned or followed in the rear, we are not told. We know only that three men made that terrible forced march.

Nothing more about the background of the thieves is said. And where the Bible is silent, a temptation is to try and fill in the back story. Here is no exception. Some early Christian writings give the thieves names. Unfortunately, the writings are not agreed on what those names were. Scholars have argued about whether these two might have been linked to Barabbas in some way since all three were sentenced to death. All of that is speculation.

Mark barely mentions the two thieves. After sharing information about the sign attached to Jesus' cross, the writer uses one sentence to say that two robbers were crucified along with Jesus, one on his right and the other on his left. John says only that two others were crucified with Jesus. He does not even call them criminals.

Matthew introduces the two in Matthew 27:38. Six verses later he says both thieves joined the priests, elders, and rulers in heaping insults on Jesus.

Luke provides the most expansive description of the two and their interactions with Jesus. His account offers different information from Matthew. Luke introduces the topic of wrongdoers during the Last Supper in the upper room. There, Luke says, Jesus quoted Isaiah 53:12, "And he was numbered with the transgressors," before adding, "I tell you that this must be fulfilled in me." (Luke 22:37).

It would not be until the next day that those who heard Jesus' words might have begun to understand them. Perhaps it was the moment they saw the thieves lined up to march with Jesus to Golgotha. Perhaps it was later, when the robbers were crucified on either side of Jesus. Perhaps it was later still when they reflected on the events related to Jesus' death. In any case, the gospel record is clear. Jesus was literally "numbered among the transgressors."

Luke alone recounts exchanges between Jesus and the thieves. From their crosses both sought Jesus' help. The first joined the jeering crowd challenging Jesus to prove he was the Christ by saving himself. Then he added, "And us." All the first thief could see in Jesus was a final chance to be rescued from execution. That "God was in Christ reconciling the world to Himself" (2 Corinthians 5:19) was something the thief's selfish spirit could not imagine.

Unlike Matthew, Luke says the second thief scolded his companion in crime saying, "Don't you fear God?" Then, for reasons unexplained, the second thief expressed faith in the Lord. "Remember me when you come into your kingdom," he asked. His words were not a demand like his partner's. Instead, they evidenced insight. Jesus was innocent. Jesus was being wrongly executed. Jesus had an attraction that went beyond the grave. With Jesus is where he wanted to be.

To such longing, Jesus responded, "Today you shall be with me in paradise" (Luke 23:43).

For Luke, Jesus was not only "numbered among the transgressors" as fulfillment of Isaiah 53:12, in his last act before committing his spirit into God's care, Jesus still drew the wayward to himself.

From the beginning of his gospel to its very end, it was important to Luke that everyone recognize that the "Son of Man came to seek and to save that which is lost" (Luke 19:10). That mission, expressed in Jesus' own words, has not changed. He still welcomes the wayward, no matter their circumstances, with the promise that "He who believes in me will live, even though he dies. And whoever lives and believes in me will never die," (John 11:25-26).

Thank you, Lord, that you welcome the wayward to yourself through faith in your atoning death on Calvary. Amen.

26

KING OF THE JEWS

"Pilate had a notice prepared and fastened to the cross. It read, 'Jesus of Nazareth, the King of the Jews.'" John 19:19

It may be surprising to many people but the only known written words about Jesus that claim to have been penned during his lifetime are the words hastily inscribed on a white gypsum board and placed atop Jesus's cross. Even then, there is not agreement on the exact wording of that sign.

History teaches that a sign or notice was prepared for each person Rome crucified. It was not enough for people to watch the torture of death on a cross. Rome wanted to make sure people knew why that person was being put to death. Often times a sign was carried in front of a prisoner as he was led to his execution. The sign was then attached to the cross so people could know why the person's life was being forfeited.

Probably the criminals crucified on either side of Jesus had a sign telling their crime, although the Bible is silent on that subject. Neither is there reference to a sign being carried in front of Jesus as he was led to Golgotha.

In John 19:19, the Bible says Pilate ordered the sign prepared. Mark 15:26 helps one recognize the normalcy of a sign when the writer says, "The written notice of the charge against him read…." There is no indication of the sign being anything but normal. Evidently, the sign was prepared at the last minute because Matthew 27:37 indicates soldiers attached the sign to Jesus' cross after he had been crucified. Attaching the sign to the cross before placing Jesus on the cross would have been easier had the sign been available.

While all four gospels share the story of the sign, there is not agreement on its exact wording. John's wording is best known. Reflected in countless Christian art pieces are the words of John's account, "Jesus of Nazareth, King of the Jews." The first letter Latin abbreviations for each word, "INRI," is widely recognized.

Matthew says the sign read, "This is Jesus, King of the Jews" (Matthew 27:37). Mark's reading is, "The King of the Jews" (Mark 15:26). Luke says the sign read, "This is the King of the Jews" (Luke 23:38). While all make the same claim, the wording inscribed on the sign is slightly different for each gospel.

Matthew says the sign was placed above Jesus' head. This has helped scholars conclude that the cross on which Jesus died was a "t" shaped cross because that was the only one of the three commonly used styles of crosses that provided a place to attach a sign above the head. John says the sign was also written in three languages – Aramaic, Latin, and Greek – to ensure that all could read the charge.

Being above the head allowed the crowd to read the sign. And when they did, it created a disturbance. John relates how the chief priests scurried back to Pilate seeking to have him change the wording. The priests were offended that the sign declared the charge as fact - "Jesus of Nazareth, King of the Jews." They asked Pilate to soften the wording to "This man claimed to be King of the Jews."

Pilate would have none of it. Instead of caving into demands from the chief priests as he had done earlier in the day, he rejected their pleadings outright. That left the chief priests in a predicament. One scholar noted that after claiming they had no king but Caesar earlier in the day, the chief priests had no choice but to accept the ruling of Caesar's representative. The sign remained.

Interestingly, the message of the sign – Jesus of Nazareth, King of the Jews - never appears in any known Christian confession. While Jesus is acknowledged as God's Messiah and is frequently referred to as king, the phrase "king of the Jews" was too limiting to be embraced by early Christians.

In Daniel 7:13-14, the Son of Man is given "authority, glory and sovereign power and all peoples, nations, and men of every language worshiped him." That theme is picked up by the author of Revelation, the last book in the Bible, who describes Jesus as "the faithful witness, the firstborn from the dead and the ruler of the kings of the earth" (Revelation 1:5).

Christian confessions acknowledge that Jesus was a Jew, that he was the Messiah, and, as such, he holds authority and power and rules over every nation and over all kings.

Pilate's sign that he had nailed on Jesus' cross was far too limited in its proclamation. Jesus is not just "king of the Jews." He is, as the author of Revelation proclaims, "King of Kings and Lord of Lords" (Revelation 19:16). That is the message of the Christian gospel.

Lord, thank you that your kingdom includes all peoples. Amen

27

GATHERED AT THE CROSS

"The people stood watching and the rulers even sneered at him."
Luke 23:35

In seven short verses, Luke describes five distinct reactions people had toward Jesus as he hung on Calvary's cross. Looking at those five reactions indicates most people today still respond to Jesus like those who witnessed his crucifixion.

Luke 23:35-41 first introduces "the people" who stood by and watched as events unfolded. This seems to be the largest number gathered to witness Jesus' death. Some of them may have been in the group that cried "crucify him" earlier that day. Some may have been among the throng that called him Messiah the previous Sunday. Some may have crowded close to Jesus as he taught in the temple during the week. Some may have been caught up in the excitement created by the merciless parade of Jesus and two others toward the site called "Place of the Skull." Like hangings in the old American West, crucifixions were sometimes community entertainment.

But now "the people" stood, perhaps with arms folded, watching the torment and suffering. Crucifixions were not uncommon. For many, they had lost their repulsion. People could observe without emotional involvement. Maybe these observers stood scrutinizing every detail so they could talk about it over supper that evening. They were just indifferent bystanders taking in what played out before them.

Perhaps those among "the people" thought the events of that day had no real bearing on them. Perhaps they thought Jesus' cross did not call for a decision or commitment. People often feel that way about the Christian faith today. Some seem to believe they can watch without being involved. That conclusion was wrong then and it is wrong today. One cannot be indifferent toward the cross. It is too important.

The priests are Luke's second group. The priests considered Jesus an imposter. How close he had come to upsetting Jerusalem's religious faithful frightened the priests. How could Jerusalem Jews have welcomed Jesus as Israel's deliverer when he arrived on Sunday, they asked themselves? How could the people have hung on his every word as he taught in the temple during the week? That kind of respect and devotion belonged to the High Priest, not a wandering teacher from Galilee, they reasoned.

Gathered around Jesus' cross, the priests gloated. Jesus was getting what he deserved. He had dared to upset the temple economy by driving vendors from temple courts (Luke 19:45). He had threatened the temple, the symbol of God's presence with the nation. Had Jesus been a true rabbi, he would have supported Jerusalem's priests, they knew. He would not have challenged them or mocked them.

Can you hear the sneers of the priests? Certain that Jesus was getting what he deserved, they scoffed, "If you are God's Messiah come down from the cross" (v.35). The cross was Jesus' "comeuppance." It proved he was wrong and they were right. Like many today, their commitment to the way things had always been blinded the priests to the new work God was doing in their midst. To contend that God must act like we want Him to or expect Him to, is a sure way to end up separated from God.

Roman soldiers had a field day with Jesus. They had heard the crowd call him "Messiah," a title reserved for the one who would drive out Rome and restore Israel's independence. They had heard Pilate, the Roman governor, refer to Jesus as "king of the Jews." Now this "king" was in their hands. Nothing would keep him for his destiny with death.

Already they had beaten him to the point that he almost died marching to Golgotha. The soldiers had to force Simon to carry Jesus' cross or Jesus might not have lived long enough to be crucified. They had belittled him with a crown of thorns and a purple robe. They had paid him false homage. Hear the antagonism in the soldiers' words at the cross, "If you are king of the Jews, save yourself" (v. 36). When the soldiers finished with Jesus, they were sure no one would dare question Roman rule. All would see nothing superseded loyalty to Rome.

For the soldiers, the power of Rome was their most important value. Like some today, what they held most dear blinded them to what was playing out before their very eyes.

On either side of Jesus was a hardened criminal condemned to die that day, too. One was so debased by life he sought only to use a dying Jesus for his own purposes. "Save yourself and us," he pleaded (v. 39). His words contained no concern for Jesus or the God Jesus served. Only selfishness and manipulation were heard as the thief sought to use Jesus for selfish ends.

Doubtless no one in hearing distance failed to understand the thief's real message: Save me. Still today people attempt to use religion for their own purposes and manipulate God for their own ends. Ultimately, it never works.

On the other side of Jesus, Luke says, a second criminal had a different response. The second thief recognized his fate was deserved. "We are getting what our deeds deserve," he said, "but this man has done nothing wrong" (v. 41).

The Bible does not tell of any previous interaction between Jesus and the second thief. Perhaps the thief had heard Jesus teach in the temple or heard people talk about him. For whatever reason, this thief asked to be remembered when Jesus "comes into your kingdom" (v. 42). In desperation the man reached out to Jesus for help. Jesus responded, "Today you will be with me in paradise" (v. 43).

Despite his past, despite his circumstances, despite his guilt, the thief reached toward Jesus and Jesus said yes. He still does.

Five reactions – the indifferent people, the sneering priests, the mocking Roman guards, the manipulating criminal, the repentant thief – each one a symbol of ways people today react to the cross of Jesus. Which one best describes your reaction to the cross?

> *Lord, forgive us when we come to you with any attitude other than to be reconciled to you through your mercy and grace. Amen.*

28

DARKNESS

"At the sixth hour darkness came over the whole land until the ninth hour." Mark 15:33

Matthew, Mark, and Luke all describe an unusual phenomenon which occurred during Jesus' time on the cross. In near identical words each says, "At the sixth hour darkness came over the whole land until the ninth hour" (Mark 15:33). The reference is not to a solar eclipse which lasts only minutes at its total eclipse stage. The gospel authors refer to something that lasted hours, something unusual with no known explanation.

Darkness is sometimes used metaphorically in the Bible, but all three synoptic writers give a specific beginning time and ending time for the darkness they report. That has led most scholars to believe the writers are describing an actual blackness that descended on the land between noon and three p.m. on the day Jesus died.

For Jews of Jesus day, darkness was filled with theological implications. Among the plagues God brought on the Egyptians was the plague of darkness (Exodus 10: 21-23). There the writer describes Moses lifting his hand toward the sky as if beckoning darkness to engulf all of Egypt. The darkness that resulted was so deep, the Bible says, it was "darkness that could be felt." So deep was the darkness that no one could see anyone else for the three days the darkness persisted. No one could see to leave where they were when the darkness fell.

Darkness is used in Exodus as a symbol of judgment on the Egyptians because the Israelites had light in the places where they lived. Darkness expressed God's anger or wrath for Pharaoh's disobedience.

But that was not Egypt's most disastrous experience with darkness. It was in the darkness of night that the death angel claimed the firstborn of every family in Egypt whose home was not protected by the blood of a lamb spread on its doorpost. Again, disobedience was the cause for God's judgment amidst the darkness. And, again, Israel was saved, this time by the blood of a Passover lamb.

Old Testament prophets continued to use darkness as a symbol of God's judgement. In Amos 8:9, the prophet discusses the Day of the Lord, a day of judgement. There he quotes God as saying, "In that day, declares the Sovereign Lord, I will make the sun go down at noon and darken the earth in broad daylight."

In Joel 2:2, the prophet describes the Day of the Lord as "a day of darkness and gloom, a day of clouds and blackness." Zephaniah offers similar words when he declared, "The day will be a day of wrath, a day of distress and anguish, a day of trouble and ruin, a day of darkness and gloom, a day of clouds and blackness" (Zephaniah 1:15).

Jeremiah uses darkness as a sign of God's changing covenant with Israel. In Jeremiah 33:19-21 the prophet quotes God as saying when Israel has broken their covenant with God to the point "that day and night no longer come at their appointed time, then my covenant…can be broken…."

All the time Jesus hung on the cross, the temple priest, scribes, and other Jewish leaders jeered at him. They challenged him to come down from the cross if he were really the son of God "so we may see and believe" (Mark 15:32). Their mocking was undeterred by the morning sun or by the unnatural darkness of the early afternoon.

They asked for a sign of their own choosing. But when darkness fell on Jerusalem at the height of the day, it was as if God gave them a sign of His choosing: darkness. As in days past, the darkness of judgment fell on sin and a system unable to save. The writer of Hebrews describes the endless sacrifices commanded by Jewish law and concludes, "This is an illustration for the present time indicating the gifts and sacrifices being offered were not able to clear the conscience of the worshiper" (Hebrews 9:9). In Hebrews 10:4, he declares, "Because it is impossible for the blood of bulls and goats to take away sin."

The darkness pointed to God's miraculous intervention in human history. Jesus, the one "despised and rejected by men," the one hanging on Calvary's cross, was God's breaking into history to offer humanity a way of escape. He was the Word of God made flesh (John 1:14) and the "light of men" (v. 4).

The darkness also spoke of deliverance. In Jesus, God was making a new covenant, not just with Israel but with all humankind. Indeed, Jeremiah's words were prophetic. At Jesus' death, the old covenant passed away. Through Jesus, a new covenant was offered to all who would believe. Jesus is the great high priest of that new covenant (Hebrews 9:11). He, also, is the Lamb of God that takes away the sins of the world. The Bible says, "He has appeared once for all at the end of the ages to do away with sin by the sacrifice of himself" (Hebrews 9:26). Also, he "did not enter by means of the blood of goats and calves, but he entered the Most Holy Place once for all by his own blood having obtained eternal redemption" (v. 12).

The purpose of it all, the writer explains, "So Christ was sacrificed once to take away the sins of many people." (v. 28).

Darkness as a sign of God's judgment. Darkness as a precursor to God's action. Darkness driven away by the light of God's mercy.

One sees all three in the story of God's deliverance of his people from physical slavery. And one sees them again in God's eternal deliverance from the darkness of sin as Jesus hung on Calvary's cross in noonday darkness.

Lord, thank you that Jesus is "the light of the world" that drives away all our darkness. Amen.

29

"NOT YET" DOESN'T MEAN "TOO LATE"

"My God, my God, why have you forsaken me?" Mark 15:34

Perhaps the most heart-wrenching prayer in the whole Bible is Jesus' final words recorded in the Gospel of Mark. Bruised and bloodied with life seeping from his body, Jesus cried, "My God, my God, why have you forsaken me?" (Mark 15:34).

Spectators around the cross failed to recognize the words as the first verse of Psalm 22. They thought Jesus cried for Elijah, that great prophet expected to reappear and prepare the way for the Jewish Messiah. Perhaps they anticipated another spectacle. "Let's see if Elijah comes and takes him down," one said.

It is striking to read Psalm 22 in light of the description of Jesus' crucifixion. In addition to Jesus praying the words of verse 1, the description of his torment is reflected in verses 6-8. The psalmist is "scorned by men and despised by the people." Remember how the crowd called for Jesus' death and jeered him as he made his way toward Golgotha?

"All who see me mock me. They hurl insults, shaking their heads." Remember the purple robe placed on Jesus shoulders in mockery?

Remember the crown of thorns and the reed scepter? Remember how he was spat upon?

Verse 8 says the people cried, "He trusts in the Lord; let the Lord rescue him." How similar to Mark 15:31 where the priests taunt Jesus with, "He saved others but himself he cannot save."

Verse 16 talks about being surrounded by evil men (the thieves on either side of Jesus) and declares "they have pierced my hands and feet."

Two verses later the psalmist writes, "They divided my garments among them and cast lots for my clothing." That is almost the exact wording of Matthew 27:35.

What prophetic foresight the psalmist had. Few can doubt the messianic overtones of this psalm and the way the death of Jesus fulfilled its vision, even the promise made in verse 24.

There the psalmist prophesied, "For He (God) has not despised or disdained the suffering of the afflicted one; He has not hidden His face from him but has listened to his cry for help."

Now on the cross Jesus cries for help and it is as if the Father answers, "Yes, but not yet."

Mark's Gospel says, "With a loud cry, Jesus breathed his last." Was God's "not yet" too late?

Mark's next two verses demonstrate that "not yet" is not the same as "too late."

Mark 15:38 records the curtain in the temple was torn in two from top to bottom the moment Jesus died. The temple contained several curtains or veils, but the wording of the Greek indicates this was "the curtain," the one that separated the Holy of Holies from the rest of the temple.

The Old Testament describes the veil as made of blue, purple, and crimson yarn and fine linen with cherubim patterns worked into the upper corners (2 Chronicles 3:14).

GETHSEMANE TO GOLGOTHA

The veil separated the place where the sins of the people could be forgiven from the rest of the temple. The High Priest could enter the holy place only once a year and then only after he had been ritually cleansed. There, on the Day of Atonement, the High Priest presented a blood offering for the sins of Israel.

Even the veil's royal colors symbolized the "otherness of God." He was God and king. He was holy, distant, and unapproachable. The veil was a barrier between God and the chosen people. It represented the ultimate separation of the clean from unclean, the foundation of the Jewish sacrificial system.

When Jesus "breathed his last," that barrier was ripped apart. In separate pieces, the veil could no longer keep people from God's presence.

Only hours before his death, Jesus shared a cup with his disciples. He said the cup represented his blood, a new covenant. Matthew 26:28 says the new covenant was "for the forgiveness of sin." The old covenant – the sacrificial system – was gone. A new covenant based on the once-for-all sacrifice of Jesus (Hebrews 10: 1-18) had taken its place.

God was no longer distant and inaccessible. Now He invited all to come to Him through becoming part of the new covenant of Jesus's shed blood. The new covenant was open to all. Jesus had paid the price for the sin of all who would believe and confess him as Lord and Savior.

The Gospel writers are unanimous in what happened Sunday morning after Jesus' death on Friday. The Father reached down into a Judean hillside where Jesus' body had been laid and raised him to new life. A new epoch in history began. The kingdom of God was glimpsed based on Jesus's blood poured out as a new covenant for the forgiveness of sin.

As prophesied in Psalm 22:24, the Father "has not despised or disdained the suffering of the afflicted one; He has not hidden His face from him but has listened to his cry for help."

Jesus' story is about victory, not about being forsaken. On the cross, Jesus was victorious over sin, over Satan, and over death itself.

To Jesus' cry about being forsaken, it is as if God answered, "Not yet." But "not yet" doesn't mean "too late."

When God answers our prayers with "not yet," may we learn to trust the one who promised "I will not leave you nor forsake you" (Hebrews 13:5).

O Lord, help us trust you no matter our circumstances. Amen.

30

THEY DIVIDED HIS CLOTHES

"When the soldiers crucified Jesus, they took his clothes, dividing them into four shares, one for each of them, with the undergarment remaining." John 19:23

Readers familiar with the time period might be surprised when reading reports in all four gospels that soldiers divided Jesus' clothes by casting lots. Typical Roman practice was to march victims to their deaths naked and then to crucify them with no clothes on at all.

But Matthew, Mark, Luke, and John all attest that Jesus wore some kind of clothing to his crucifixion. And it was what he wore those soldiers divided among themselves. Perhaps it was a concession to Jewish modesty that Rome allowed Jewish victims to wear some kind of clothing. While there was not unanimity among Jewish scholars about whether one who is stoned to death for blasphemy could be naked, one Midrash statement contends, "One of the most shameful things in the world is to be punished naked in the marketplace."

For whatever reason, Mark 15:20 clearly states that after the Roman soldiers mocked and abused Jesus, they put his own clothes on him before parading him through Jerusalem to the place of crucifixion. After the crucifixion, the soldiers divided items such as his headgear, sandals, girdle, and tunic. Mark says there was something for each of the soldiers but does not say how many soldiers there were. John says there were four.

Matthew, Mark, and Luke say the soldiers cast lots to determine what each soldier would receive. John presents a slightly different narrative. In John 19:23-24, the writer reports the soldiers divided Jesus clothes into four shares so each would get something. He does not mention how the divisions were made.

John says there was one garment left, a seamless, woven garment of one piece from top to bottom. In Greek, the garment is called a chiton. It is the same word used to describe Joseph's "coat of many colors." The implication is not that Jesus' garment was many-colored, but it was an unusual garment. Perhaps, like Joseph's coat, the garment marked Jesus as special, as chosen. Indeed, John saw Jesus as God's chosen one, the Messiah.

Others see the chiton as pointing to the priestly role of Jesus. In Exodus 39:27, the seamless chiton is one of the garments worn by the high priest. Some early Christians saw John's description of the soldiers not tearing the garment in pieces as pointing back to Leviticus 21:10 which specifies that the high priest's chiton could not be torn.

Some see in John's story symbolism that points to Jesus as the true high priest. Certainly, the early church understood Jesus to be that and more. Hebrews 9 is filled with such imagery. In verse 11, Jesus is called "high priest." He entered the Most Holy Place (v. 12), a place reserved only for the high priest. He offered the blood sacrifice which was the responsibility of the high priest. As high priest, he was mediator between God and man (v. 15).

But Jesus was more than high priest. He was the offering itself. Again, verse 12, "But he entered the Most Holy Place once for all by his own blood having obtained eternal redemption." Verse 14, "How much more then, will the blood of Christ, who through the eternal Spirit offered himself unblemished to God, cleanse our consciences from acts that lead to death...." Verse 26, "Now he has appeared once for all at the end of the ages to do away with sin by the sacrifice of himself."

Whether the symbolism was intended or not, the word John used for Jesus' seamless garment evokes connections that are not only interesting but true. Jesus is both God's Chosen One and our Great High Priest.

This is not by accident, as John makes clear in verse 24. After describing the decision not to tear the woven garment, John writes, "This happened that the scripture might be fulfilled."

Centuries earlier in a Davidic psalm associated with the longed-for Messiah, the psalmist wrote, "They divided my garments among them and cast lots for my clothing," (Psalm 22:18). Matthew, Mark, and Luke all point toward the fulfillment of that verse with their accounts of soldiers casting lots to decide how Jesus' clothes would be divided.

But John goes farther than hinting. His description fulfills both statements of the psalm. The soldiers divided Jesus' garments and they cast lots for his clothes. This, he declares, was evidence of God's guiding hand in the life and work of Jesus even down to such small details as dividing his clothes.

Lord, give us eyes to see how you are working in history to bring all people to yourself. Amen.

31

PROTESTING JESUS' DEATH

"When all the people who had gathered to witness this sight saw what took place, they beat their breasts and went away." Luke 23:48

A protest doesn't have to be a riot. It doesn't have to be violent and lawless. A protest, by definition, can be an expression of disapproval. Certainly, there were those who expressed their disapproval of Jesus' crucifixion.

Luke 23:24 presents a large crowd who followed Jesus to Golgotha including a large number of women. This crowd does not appear to be the same people who earlier called for Jesus' crucifixion for the women in this crowd loudly wailed and mourned for Jesus. They were protesting his death sentence as they acted out their grief.

So prominent was their protest that Jesus noticed it. He stopped and addressed the "daughters of Jerusalem" with grim descriptions of what awaited the city because Israel consistently rejected God's messengers and killed the prophets.

But Jesus' warning did not stop the women from continuing their protests up to the moment that Jesus died. In verse 48, the writer lets us know that not only the women but "all the people" who witnessed Jesus' death went away "beating their breasts." Whether the writer intended to include the priests and Pharisees in this group is doubtful.

Beating one's breast was a sign of remorse, contrition, anguish, and grief. Earlier in Luke 18:9-14, Jesus told the story of a Pharisee and a tax collector who offered prayers to God. The tax collector was so convicted of his unworthiness that he "beat his breast" (v. 13) in contrition.

Now many who saw Jesus die protested what had happened by beating their breasts.

An early non-biblical writing called Acts of Pilate reflects on this scene when it reports, "Now, as the governor looked around on the multitudes of the Jews standing around, he saw many of the Jews weeping, and said, 'Not all the multitude wish that he should be put to death.'"

There were followers of Jesus who protested his death by their presence at the foot of the cross. John 19:25-27 reports the presence of Mary, the mother of Jesus, her sister Mary, wife of Clopas, and Mary Magdalene together with the "disciple whom Jesus loved," usually identified as John.

Luke adds that "all those who knew him (Jesus), including the women who had followed him from Galilee, stood watching these things" (Luke 19:49).

Some at the cross, like the priests, sneered at Jesus. Some mocked him - the soldiers. The unrepentant thief and others blasphemed. But amidst all the evil, there was a remnant who protested, mourned, and grieved.

The Old Testament prophet Zechariah foresaw such a time. In Zechariah 12:10, he wrote, "They will look on me, the one they have pierced, and they will mourn for him as one mourns for an only child and grieve bitterly for him as one grieves for a firstborn son."

Unintended as it may have been, the events surrounding Jesus' death fulfilled this ancient prophesy. And while unintended by human hands, the circumstances around Jesus' death fulfilled all that was intended for the Lamb of God who was chosen before the creation of the world to bring salvation to all who believe on his name (1 Peter 1:20).

Lord, like those who mourned Jesus' death at the cross, let us be faithful to you, even when we have to stand against the crowd. Amen.

32

THE MINISTRY OF PRESENCE

"Many other women who had come up with him to Jerusalem were also there." Mark 15:41b

John Milton ended his famous poem "On His Blindness" with the immortal words, "They also serve who only stand and wait." Though intended as affirmation of his place in God's world despite his blindness, Milton's words have comforted countless folk across the centuries whose primary contribution has been to "stand and wait." They served by being present.

That could be said of the group of women who faithfully followed Jesus even as he hung on a cross and beyond.

Matthew, Mark, and Luke all confirm that a group of Jesus-following women stood at a distance and helplessly watched as Jesus was crucified (Matthew 27:55, Mark 15:40, Luke 23:49). The gospel writers agree these were women from Galilee. Mark says that in Galilee these women had followed Jesus and cared for his needs. Matthew adds the women had followed Jesus to Jerusalem in order to continue caring for him. Some scholars believe the Greek vocabulary used by the gospel writers indicates these women may have financially supported Jesus from their own resources.

If true, it would not be surprising. The disciples hardly supported themselves by doing odd jobs as they traveled during the three years of Jesus' public ministry.

A few of the women are named: Mary Magdalene; Mary, the mother of James and Joses; Salome; and Mary, the wife of Clopas. Most are anonymous. Nothing is said about how they came to faith in Jesus or about the service they offered him and the disciples. We know nothing about their hopes concerning what might happen when Jesus arrived in Jerusalem. Perhaps they dared to dream of Israel being restored and Rome driven from their Jewish homeland. That was a popular longing among most Jews.

Instead, Jewish officials manipulated circumstances to the point that Rome was now crucifying the one they followed. Rome even mocked Jesus with a crude white sign calling him "King of the Jews."

But regardless of their personal despair and despite their broken dreams, these women stood on the edge of the hostile crowd and watched as physical life ebbed from Jesus' tortured body. The disciples were in hiding, fearing they might be arrested and put to death. But the faithful band of women who had cared for Jesus in Galilee and followed him to Jerusalem was there. They could not change the circumstances, but they could serve by being a presence.

Anyone who has suffered the loss of a loved one knows it is not necessarily the words of friends that brings solace and comfort in such moments. It is their loving presence. Caring friends are there to walk with the grieving and share in the suffering, as much as possible. They serve by standing at one's side and simply being present. They wait.

When Joseph of Arimathea placed Jesus' body in his own newly hewn sepulcher, Luke reports, "The women who had followed Jesus from Galilee followed Joseph and saw the tomb and how his body was laid in it" (Luke 23:55). Matthew and Mark report that only Mary Magdalene and the other Mary saw where Jesus was buried. John does not mention anyone observing the burial.

Continuing his story, Luke says on the first day of the week, the women took spices to wrap in Jesus' burial cloths to help mask the odor of decay. The other gospels list specific individuals. That Luke means more than the named individuals is affirmed in Luke 24:10, where, after listing the commonly named women, Luke adds, "and the others with them." Although unnamed, they were still there.

Matthew, Mark, and John each report an encounter between the women who went to the grave on Sunday morning and Jesus, though each account contains slight differences from the others. But Luke's gospel is silent about an encounter between the risen Jesus and those who served by standing and waiting. When one reads Luke's second volume, the Book of Acts, the situation changes. In Acts 13:31, Luke recounts a sermon by the Apostle Paul in which Paul declared, "And for many days he (Jesus) was seen by those who had traveled with him from Galilee to Jerusalem."

Not only did the women who traveled with him to Jerusalem see Jesus, Luke writes that he was seen "many days" by this group. Then Luke adds, "They are now his witnesses to our people."

Again, the women are mostly an anonymous group of individuals. How they cared for Jesus in Galilee is a matter of speculation and interpretation. What they did for him in Jerusalem is unknown. Whether Jesus knew these followers watched from the edge of the crowd while he was crucified will never be known. They saw him and, perhaps, he saw them. Interestingly, Psalms 38:11 says in the Modern English Version, "My friends and my companions stand back because of my affliction, and those close to me stand at a distance."

Even in the darkest moments, the women were there. They could not change the circumstances, but they could exercise the ministry

BOBBY S. (BOB) TERRY

of presence. Like Milton's imaginary soldiers, they served the Lord by standing and waiting. In doing so, they became "his witnesses to our people," as Paul called them.

Lord, thank you for what you can do with those who faithfully serve by standing and waiting. Amen.

33

I COMMIT MY SPIRIT

> "Jesus called out with a loud voice, 'Father, into your hands I commit my spirit.' When he had said this, he breathed his last."
> Luke 23:46

According to the gospel of Luke, Jesus' last words came from a psalm. In Luke 23:46, the writer quotes Jesus as saying, "Father, into your hands I commit my spirit." That quote comes from Psalm 31:5. Psalm 31 is a cry for deliverance from one's enemies. It is also a psalm that expresses trust in God. The psalmist describes God as his refuge, his rock, his fortress, and his guide.

With that kind of confidence, it is not surprising for the psalmist to pray "into your hands I commit my spirit."

Jesus personalized that prayer by addressing God as "Father." It was the same reference Jesus used in the Garden of Gethsemane as the fateful events related to his death began to unfold. It was Luke's way of showing readers that even though God did not grant Jesus' request of "this cup be taken from me," Jesus understood that God was still his Father.

The physical pain he endured, the loneliness and betrayal he experienced, the emotional distress he bore, not even the darkness that surrounded him as he died – none of these could change Jesus' confidence and trust in his Father.

Earlier Luke wrote of Jesus being "betrayed into the hands of men" (Luke 9:44). But no one could take Jesus' life from him. He laid it down of his own free will. And when he did lay it down, it was into the hands of the Father that he committed his spirit.

Spirit is not a component of a human being like some organ of the body. Spirit is a reference to all that one is. One scholar wrote that spirit is, "The living self or life power that goes beyond death."

For Jesus, spirit included even more. Jesus alone was conceived by the spirit according to Luke 1:35. The verse is not a reference to a sex act but rather calls to mind the creative power of God referenced in the creation story of Genesis 1.

As Jesus began his public ministry with baptism, the spirit descended on him in the bodily form of a dove (Luke 3:22). Then God announced, "This is my beloved son with whom I am well pleased." That spirit enlivened Jesus' ministry from beginning to end.

Luke 4:1 describes Jesus as "full of the spirit" and then recounts how Jesus could withstand the temptations of Satan himself because of the presence of God's spirit. Verse 14 of that chapter describes how the power of the spirit guided Jesus in all that he did.

The Bible is clear. Jesus was given human life by the spirit. His ministry was enlivened by the spirit. He was empowered by the spirit and guided by the spirit. At the center of his being and his ministry was the spirit.

At the end of his days, when he had fulfilled his purpose of establishing a new covenant which offered salvation to humankind, Jesus could confidently commit his spirit to the Father. He could reach back to a psalm of David. Surrounded by enemies who sought to destroy him, he could pray, "Father, into your hands I commit my spirit."

Luke's account magnifies what trust Jesus had in the Father.

Early Christians did not miss the significance of that prayer. As they, in turn, faced martyrdom, they often followed Jesus' example. Acts 7:59 tells the story of Stephen. With life ebbing from his body because of the stones hurled upon him, he knelt and prayed, "Lord Jesus, receive my spirit." With confident trust in God, he walked into death knowing God was there to receive him.

When my late wife died and I stood by the open grave watching her casket slowly descending into the earth, my prayer was, "Lord, into your hands I commit her spirit." That was possible only because years earlier she had committed herself to God through faith in Jesus Christ. Because she had made that decision, I could echo her words knowing that "the life power that goes beyond the grave" can be trusted into God's care.

Thank you, Lord, that at the end of our lives you are there to receive our spirits because of trusting faith in Jesus. Amen.

34

THE CURTAIN IN THE TEMPLE

"At that moment the curtain of the temple was torn in two from top to bottom. The earth shook and the rocks split." Matthew 27:51

While slight differences will be found on when the "curtain in the temple" was torn in two, all three synoptic gospels record that decisive event. Luke says the curtain was torn in two right before Jesus died (Luke 23:45). Mark says that Jesus breathed his last and then the curtain was torn in two from top to bottom (Mark 15:37-38). Matthew is more specific. He says at the moment Jesus "gave up his spirit," the curtain of the temple was torn in two from top to bottom (Matthew 27:51).

All three writers describe the event with a passive verb indicating that something was done to the curtain. It did not tear by itself. Matthew is the only one who offers an explanation for it tearing when he writes "the earth shook, and the rocks split" when Jesus died. Evidently, earthquakes shook the area.

The English translation "torn" obscures the impact of the Greek word used by Matthew and Mark. More appropriate may be a term like "ripped" to show the aggressive nature of what happened to the curtain. Several scholars combine the aggressiveness of the Greek verb and its passive voice to show that God was the one who ripped the curtain into pieces.

For Christians, the ripped curtain is a symbol of hope. For the Jews, it was a sign of punishment.

Jewish leaders refused to heed Jesus' message to "repent for the kingdom of God is at hand." More than refusing to heed the message, they actively opposed the messenger, seeking to undermine him with the people. When that did not work, they sought to kill him. True to its reputation as "the city that kills the prophets," (Luke 13:34), leaders helped kill the messenger in order to silence the message.

That morning on the march to Calvary, Jesus had warned of the coming destruction of the city because of its rebellion against God (Luke 23: 28-31). But the pending doom was more than the physical destruction of the city. It was also the end of the temple and all it represented.

Early Christians saw the resurrection of Jesus as the beginning of a new covenant between God and humanity based on what happened on the cross. And when future Roman Emperor Titus led the Roman army to destroy Jerusalem on September 8, 70 AD, they saw it as the punishment Jesus foretold for Jerusalem on the morning he died. Both were tied to the curtain of the temple being ripped in pieces.

The curtain of the temple described the curtain separating the Holy of Holies from the rest of the Jewish temple. Leviticus 16:11-19 describes how the High Priest entered that sacred space only once a year on the Day of Atonement. There he offered blood sacrifices for his own sin and for the sins of the people. But when the curtain was torn apart, the holy character of the space was destroyed. And with it went the old way through which God related to humankind.

Using the imagery of Leviticus 16:11-19, it is as if the sacrifice which began on the cross was continued as Jesus took the sacrifice of his own blood into the highest heavens and presented it as an eternal offering for sin.

That is what the writer of Hebrews affirms. Hebrews 4:14 reads, "Therefore, since we have a great high priest who has gone through the heavens, Jesus, the Son of God." Hebrews 5: 9 adds, "He became the source of salvation for all who obey him." Hebrews 9:12, declares, "He entered the Most Holy Place once for all by his own blood having obtained eternal redemption." Hebrews 9:24 continues, "For Christ did not enter a man-made sanctuary that was only a copy of the true one. He entered heaven itself, now to appear for us in God's presence…. But now he has appeared once for all at the end of the ages to do away with sin by the sacrifice of himself" (v. 26).

What the gospel writers teach through the symbol of the curtain being ripped apart, the writer of Hebrews explains in detail.

During Jesus' trial before the Sanhedrin, false witnesses swore Jesus had said he would destroy the Jerusalem temple and rebuild it in three days (Mark 14:58). In a totally unexpected way, that testimony proved true. With the death of Jesus on the cross, the purpose of the Jerusalem temple was destroyed. Awaiting fulfillment was only the second half of that testimony: that in three days another temple would appear.

Resurrection hope broke forth on Sunday when Jesus was "declared with power to be the Son of God" (Romans 1:4). He was the Great High Priest. He was the one through whose blood forgiveness was offered. He was the first fruit, the hope of the world.

But, on Good Friday when Jesus became obedient unto death, God declared the price of salvation paid. And He signaled it to all when He ripped the curtain of the temple in two from top to bottom.

Lord, thank You for acting to save us from sin once for all through Jesus. Amen.

35

THE CENTURION'S CONFESSION

"When the centurion who stood there in front of Jesus heard his cry and saw how he died, he said, 'Surely this man was the Son of God.'" Mark 14: 39

Near the conclusion of the Golgotha event is one of the most ironic moments of the whole story. With Jesus' lifeless body still hanging on the cross, the centurion leader of the Roman soldiers who crucified Jesus confessed, "Truly, this was the son of God."

The gospels of Matthew, Mark, and Luke all share the story. The centurion who supervised the Roman soldiers as they mocked and belittled Jesus, the one who led the soldiers in beating Jesus to the point he was unable to carry his cross to the execution site, the one who directed the crucifixion, the one whom Pilate called to confirm that Jesus was dead – this was the one who concluded that Jesus really was the son of God.

The irony doesn't stop there. During his trial before the Sanhedrin, Caiaphas, the Jewish High Priest, asked if Jesus was "the Christ, the son of God" (Matthew 26:63). When Jesus answered, "Yes, it is as you say," Caiaphas and most other Sanhedrin members accused Jesus of blasphemy. They said he should die for such a claim. Yet hours later, a Roman soldier – a gentile – confessed that Jesus was who he claimed to be, the son of God.

Matthew goes beyond both Mark and Luke at this point. Matthew says all the soldiers who guarded Jesus joined in that confession (Matthew 27:54). Jesus' own people could not see the truth, but gentiles could. The Sanhedrin elite condemned him. The common Roman soldier recognized him as God's son.

Luke words the centurion's confession differently from the other two gospels. In Luke 23:47, one reads, "This was a righteous man." A better translation, most scholars agree, would be "This was the Righteous One" which is equivalent to "son of God." The Roman soldiers were not attesting to Jesus being a good person or innocent of charges made against him. Their declaration was that Jesus was "the son of God." It has the same weight as Peter's confession at Caesarea Philippi when he said, "You are the Christ, the son of the Living God."

What caused such a conversion in the attitude of the centurion and soldiers toward Jesus? Luke says "seeing what had happened" the centurion began praising God (Luke 23:47). Mark says it was after hearing Jesus' cry to God and seeing how he died (Mark 15:39). Matthew says it was after "seeing the earthquake and all that had happened," a reference to the darkness that descended on the area from noon to about 3:00 p.m., the earthquake, rocks rent, tombs opened and other eschatological signs (Matthew 27:54).

For whatever reason, Jesus became "light" in the spiritually dark gentile world just as predicted at his birth. Luke relates that when Jesus was taken to the temple to be dedicated to God through the act of circumcision, a spirit-filled man named Simeon took Jesus in his arms praying, "My eyes have seen your salvation, which you have prepared in the sight of all people, a light for revelation to the gentiles and for the glory of your people" (Luke 2: 30-32).

Matthew develops this theme further as he emphasizes God reaching out to all people through Jesus from his birth to his death. Matthew recounts that at his birth, the Jewish King Herod the Great, with information provided by the chief priests and teachers of the law, tried to kill Jesus. At the same time, it was the Wise Men from other nations and other ethnicities who came to worship Jesus as "king of the Jews."

Now, at the end of his earthly life, it was still Jews who schemed to put Jesus to death, and it was gentiles who confessed him as son of God.

Each of the three synoptic gospels carry this theme through to its final verses where Jesus directed the message of salvation is to be preached to all people in every nation.

Perhaps Jesus hinted at this outcome earlier when, after encountering another centurion who had faith in him, said, "I say to you that many will come from the east and the west and will take their places at the feast with Abraham, Isaac, and Jacob in the kingdom of heaven. But the subjects of the kingdom will be thrown outside into the darkness" (Matthew 8: 11-12).

Neither the centurion nor the Roman soldiers with him had a thousand-year history of worshiping the One True God like the Jews did. They did not have a heritage of prophets and prophecies. They did not have a culture with God at the center of life. But when they saw the signs in the heavens (darkness), signs on earth (earthquakes and rent rocks), and signs under the earth (opened tombs and more), they saw the awesome power of God at work. They had heard Jesus cry out about being forsaken by God, but they interpreted "all that had happened" as evidence that God had not forsaken the one nailed to the cross.

Their confession, "this was the son of God," was not some sarcastic, cynical question like "this was the son of God?" No. It was a full-throated affirmation that "Truly (or Surely) this was the son of God."

At the foot of the cross, the confessing centurion and the soldiers with him are an unmistakable symbol of God's intention of reaching out with the gospel to all people everywhere.

Dear Lord, help us faithfully proclaim salvation through Jesus to all people everywhere. Amen

36

WHO IS RESPONSIBLE?

> "You…are determined to make us (the Sanhedrin) guilty of this man's blood." Acts 5:28

Who is responsible for the death of Jesus? That is a question Christians have argued for centuries. It is a question argued in the days following Jesus' death, burial, resurrection, and ascension. Acts 5 tells the story of an argument between the Sanhedrin and the Apostles over this very issue.

The Apostles were accused of being "determined to make us (the Sanhedrin) guilty of this man's blood" (v. 28). Peter answers defiantly, "The God of our Fathers raised Jesus from the dead – whom you had killed by hanging him on a tree" (v. 30).

Peter's statement reflects the position of the early church. The Sanhedrin – the chief priests, elders, and teachers of the law – sought to have Jesus killed. They may not have committed the actual deed, but Jesus' crucifixion was their idea.

That understanding is consistent with Matthew's gospel. It was the chief priests and elders who "persuaded the crowd" to have Jesus executed (Matthew 27:20). It was under the leadership of the chief priests and elders that the crowd cried, "his blood on us and our children" (v. 25) – a way of accepting responsibility for what was about to take place.

Often Christians stop with the conclusion that the Jews killed Jesus. But there may be additional information to inform our understanding. For example, Judas, a former disciple of Jesus, bears some responsibility. It was Judas who took the initiative to seek out the chief priests about betraying Jesus. It was Judas who led the arresting party to the place where Jesus prayed. Without Judas' actions, Jesus would not have been arrested that night. He would not have been tried and would not have died on Passover's Preparation Day.

Certainly, the chief priests, elders, and teachers of the law bear responsibility. It was Caiaphas, the Jewish High Priest, who contended it was better for one man (Jesus) to die than to risk Rome's wrath on the nation (John 11:50). It was members of the Sanhedrin who sought false testimony to convict Jesus after his arrest (Matthew 26:59, 66). It was the High Priest who charged Jesus with blasphemy, a crime worthy of death in Jewish law (Leviticus 24:10-16).

Pilate cannot escape his role in Jesus' death despite his attempts to reject responsibility. Some argue Pilate tried to follow his wife's advice and not get involved with Jesus' destiny. Others contend the Roman governor followed practices outlined in Deuteronomy 21:1-9 when he washed his hands symbolizing his rejection of any part in Jesus's death.

Contrary to the guidance of Deuteronomy, Pilate did know about the death of Jesus. He had knowledge about innocent blood being shed. Washing his hands could not wash away his responsibility of consenting to the crucifixion and authorizing Roman soldiers to carry out the sentence.

And then there was the crowd, called "all the people" in Matthew 27:25. Some see the phrase as a deliberate effort to tie Jesus' death back to Leviticus 24. That Old Testament passage declares that anyone who blasphemes the name of God must be put to death by the whole community" (v. 16).

The Sanhedrin convicted Jesus of blasphemy. The chief priests and elders convinced the crowd that Jesus was a blasphemer worthy of death. Now "all the people" – the community, the entire assembly – accepted its responsibility to put the blasphemer to death in accordance with Scripture teaching.

The conclusion is inescapable. Those numbered among the crowd that day bear responsibility for Jesus' death, too.

There is more.

In the Upper Room at what is called The Lord's Supper, Jesus held out the wine cup and said, "This is my blood of the covenant which is poured out for many for the forgiveness of sin" (Matthew 26:28). The analogy was to the Day of Atonement (Yom Kippur). In biblical times, blood offerings were poured out in the Holy of Holies as an offering to take away the sins of Israel.

In the last hours of his life, Jesus identifies himself as a sin offering poured out for the forgiveness of sin. As John the Baptist earlier declared, Jesus was "the Lamb of God who takes away the sins of the world" (John 1:29).

Jesus' blood was poured out to "take away the sins of the world." Not just the sins of Jews but the sins of all. That means sin was responsible for Jesus' death as well. My sin. Your sin. The sin of all. We all played a part in Jesus' death because we all "have sinned and come short of the glory of God" (Romans 3:23).

Ultimately, we are responsible for Jesus' death because it was for our sin that he died on the cross.

Lord, thank you for your mercy and grace poured out on sinners like me who caused Jesus to die on Calvary's tree. Amen.

37

NOT AN ACCIDENTAL DEATH

"Jesus died for our sins according to the scripture…." 1 Corinthians 15:3.

Jesus' death was not an accident in history. It was not as if a runaway team of horses unexpectedly trampled him on some Jerusalem street. The message of the early church was that "Jesus died for our sins according to the scripture…" (1 Corinthians 15:3). His death was purposeful and full of meaning for all humankind.

It was not accidental that Jesus was crucified on Friday, the preparation day for Sabbath worship in Jewish life. But it was not any Friday. It was the preparation day for a special Sabbath – Passover. That day recalled the long-ago event during Egyptian captivity when the Death Angel passed over all the Jewish homes marked with the blood of a sacrificial lamb. It was the day God brought freedom to the Jewish slaves. Now, centuries later, the one an angel said would "save his people from their sins" (Matthew 1:21) was about to usher in a new kind of freedom - freedom from the punishment of sin.

Each of the synoptic gospels affirms that darkness descended on the area around the sixth hour (noon). That timing was not by chance. Noon was the time the Jewish priest began sacrificing the Passover lambs at the temple. And, as the priest slew the unblemished lambs and poured their blood on the bonfire as a sacrifice to God, Jesus' blood trickled from his wounds at the Place of the Skull. It was certainly a dark time.

For the writer of the Gospel of John, it was important to demonstrate that Jesus died "according to the scripture." He describes the guards dividing Jesus' belongings as Jesus hung on the cross. The writer points out the gambling fulfilled the prophecy of Psalms 22:18, "They divided my clothes among them and cast lots for my clothing."

John also adds details not found in the other gospels. He recounts the Jews asking that the legs of the crucified be broken to hasten their deaths since it was against Jewish law for one to hang on a tree during the Sabbath. Pilate consented but the soldiers did not break Jesus' legs because he was already dead. Again, John points out that this fulfilled a scripture prophesy. Speaking of God's chosen, Psalm 34:21 declares that "not one of his bones shall be broken."

Instead, a soldier plunged his spear into Jesus' side. Once more John points to scripture fulfillment. Zachariah 12:10, declares, "They shall look on me, the one they have pierced."

That the writer of John saw the death of Jesus as fulfilling scripture is assured. But Jesus' death was more than that. With the description of blood and water flowing from the spear wound in Jesus' side (John 19:34), John affirms that Jesus' death was both sacrificial and life giving. So important is this point that the writer offers a witness to its veracity. In John 19:35, the writer says, "The man who saw it gives testimony and his testimony is true." The writer then adds the purpose of this testimony is "that you may believe." Obviously, seeing the blood and water flowing from Jesus was important.

Scholars generally agree the blood flowing from Jesus' side symbolized his death. Jewish law indicated that at the moment of death, the blood of the sacrificial lamb was to be captured and sprinkled on those seeking forgiveness before the rest being offered to God as a burnt offering. Similarly, in death, the blood of Jesus flowed from his body as an offering to God for the sins of all humankind who believe in Jesus.

John the Baptist called Jesus "the Lamb of God that takes away the sins of the world" (John 1:29). Jesus himself taught that he came into the world to "give himself a ransom for many" (Mark 10:45). On the cross, the words of Jesus, as well as the prophecies of John the Baptist, became reality.

It is no wonder the message of the early church continues today. Jesus "is the atoning sacrifice for our sins but not only ours but for the sins of the whole world" (1 John 2:2).

Water symbolized the life-giving impact of Jesus' death.

Water was a symbol of life in the parched environment of Jesus' surroundings. In John 7:38, Jesus promised that all who believe in him will have "streams of living water" flow from them. The gospel writer offers commentary on Jesus' words. He adds, "By this he meant the spirit, whom those who believed on him were later to receive." The writer adds that the spirit would not be given until Jesus was "glorified."

But in his death Jesus was glorified (John 12:23-24). He was the "lamb of God." He had been "lifted up from the earth" and paid sin's price. Now he could draw all men unto himself (v. 32). Not only would believers receive forgiveness, they also would receive the life-giving spirit of God. It would be available to all and for all times. As Zachariah 13:1 promised, "On that day a fountain will be open to the house of David and the inhabitants of Jerusalem...." That spirit is described in the prior chapter as a spirit of grace and compassion.

No one fully understands the economy of God but in the death of Jesus, God's only begotten son, the righteousness of God was demonstrated as God himself both demanded the price and paid the price for sin – your sin and mine.

No, nothing about Jesus' death was accidental. It was according to the scriptures in its details and in its purpose. Through the death of Jesus all who believe are justified before God and all who believe are given life eternal.

Lord, thank you that you acted to provide salvation for all who will believe in the atoning death of Jesus. Amen.

38

MORE ON WHO IS RESPONSIBLE FOR JESUS' DEATH

"Father, forgive them for they do not know what they are doing."
Matthew 5:44

As Jesus hung from the cross, Luke's gospel says his first words were, "Father, forgive them for they do not know what they are doing," (Luke 23:34). Those words are consistent with the character Jesus demonstrated during his years of public ministry. In the Sermon on the Mount, Jesus taught that one should "love your enemies and pray for those who persecute you" (Matthew 5:44). Now, in his last hours, Jesus lived out that commitment.

But for whom did Jesus offer his prayer of forgiveness? Was it for Judas who broke Jesus' heart when he sacrificed a personal relationship for monetary gain? Was it for the religious leaders who lied and manipulated those around them to accomplish their personal agenda? Was it for Pilate who tried to cover his personal insecurity with violence? Was it for the crowd who days before called him Messiah but now labeled him a blasphemer? Was it for you and me – sinners whose debt he willingly paid that fateful day in Jerusalem?

The answer to that question is more than an esoteric exercise. The answer lies at the base of one of history's tragedies – persecution of Jews as Christ killers.

Origen, an early Church Father, reflected on the crowd's agreement that "his blood on us and our children" and concluded, "For this reason the blood of Jesus is not only on those who lived at that moment but on all the generations of Jews that followed till the end of time." Unfortunately, others in Christian history agreed with that conclusion.

Through the centuries some Christians have acted as if Jesus never prayed, "Father, forgive them…" and as if his prayer did not include the Jews involved in his crucifixion. Such a view makes God's wrath eternal and his mercy momentary.

The psalmist offers an opposing view. Psalms 136 echoes the cry "his mercy endures forever" in every one of its 28 verses. Psalm 118 begins with the affirmation that God's "mercy endures forever." In Psalms 100:5, the writer declares, "For the Lord is good and his mercy endures forever; his faithfulness continues through all generations."

This is the God who through Jesus teaches to love one's enemies, to forgive them 70 times seven and on the cross prayed, "Father forgive them for they do not know what they are doing."

It is God's wrath, his anger, which "lasts only a moment" (Psalms 30:5).

Leviticus 24:10-16 provides understanding for this issue. There the Law of Moses commands that a blasphemer be put to death by the whole community or assembly. The Sanhedrin convicted Jesus of blasphemy (Matthew 26:65). The chief priests, elders, and teachers of the law then convinced the crowd that Jesus was a blasphemer and should be put to death.

A parallel in today's society might be a jury sentencing an innocent person to death based on manufactured evidence presented by a dishonest prosecutor. The cry "his blood on us and our children" was like members of the jury affirming their verdict when polled by the judge. Both are ways of accepting responsibility for the outcome.

Neither justifies the conclusion of responsibility on "all generations...that follow until the end of time," as Origen wrote. Death was what the law required in each instance and death is what the crowd and the jury supported.

Origen's idea of inherited guilt "for all generations...to the end of time" is contrary to what God said through the prophet Jeremiah. In Jeremiah 31: 29 – 30, the prophet spoke for God, declaring, "In those days people will no longer say, 'The fathers have eaten sour grapes and the children's teeth are set on edge.' Instead, everyone will die for his own sin. Whoever eats sour grapes, his own teeth will be set on edge."

When Peter preached at Pentecost, he preached to a largely Jewish audience. He did not shy away from naming the role his listeners played in Jesus' death (see Acts 5:23). Yet, he proclaimed forgiveness for all.

Scholars generally agree early Christians saw Rome's sack of Jerusalem in 70 AD as fulfillment of Jesus' prophecy in Luke 23:28-31 on his way to the cross and as God's punishment for the Jews crucifying Jesus. At the same time, scholars also agree that the Apostle Paul and other early Christian leaders longed for the day that Jews en masse would believe in Jesus as the true Messiah (Romans 9-11).

Until that day dawns, perhaps Christian believers should give thanks for Jesus beseeching God's forgiveness for all responsible for his death on the cross. Perhaps we should imitate our Lord by offering a similar prayer for ourselves and for others.

And, perhaps we should focus on incarnating God's mercy and love as we live with one another and leave expressions of wrath to the One who judges us all.

Lord, may Your love for all people be evidenced by the way Christian believers live with others in our world which so desperately needs the good news of Jesus. Amen.

39

WITNESSES TO JESUS' BURIAL

"The women who had come with Jesus from Galilee followed Joseph and saw the tomb and how his body was laid in it." Luke 23:55

Sometimes Christians assume Jesus' burial was done almost secretly. The gospels say the opposite. Matthew, Mark, and Luke all report that Jesus' followers saw where he was buried. In John's gospel, Mary Magdalene knew where the tomb was though nothing is said about how she knew.

Matthew 27:55 says many women watched from a distance as Jesus died. Verse 66 adds that Mary Magdalene and "the other Mary" were actually sitting opposite the tomb Joseph of Arimathea used to bury Jesus. That account lends credence to the tomb being close to Golgotha. Mark 15:40 names three women who watched Jesus' burial - Mary Magdalene, Mary the mother of James the Younger and of Joses, and Salome. The next verse adds that "many other women…were also there." Luke 23:55, reports that "women who had come with Jesus from Galilee followed Joseph and saw the tomb and how Jesus body was laid in it."

GETHSEMANE TO GOLGOTHA

Jewish officials also knew where Jesus was buried. Matthew describes how the chief priests from the temple, together with the Pharisees, asked Pilate to place guards around the tomb to make sure no one stole Jesus' body (Matthew 27:62-63). Obviously, the Jews knew where they wanted the soldiers stationed.

Romans also knew where Jesus was buried because Pilate sent guards who sealed the tomb and then stood guard around it day and night. (Matthew 27:65).

All four gospels report that around dawn on the first day of the week, some women went to Jesus' tomb. The lists of these women contain slight differences. In John, Mary Magdalene went alone. Matthew says Mary Magdalene was accompanied by one other. In Mark, she is accompanied by two others. Luke offers an indefinite number. Luke 24:10, reads, "it was Mary Magdalene, Joanna, Mary the mother of James, and the others with them who told this."

No matter the number of women visiting the tomb that morning, all four gospels report they found an empty tomb.

Matthew offers the most dramatic description of that morning. There one reads that as the women neared the tomb, there was an earthquake. Then an angel descended, went to the tomb, rolled away the stone and sat on it. So frightening was the experience, the Roman guards fell to the ground and "became as dead men" (Matthew 28:4). The angel, whose appearance was described as "like lightning" and whose clothes were "as white as snow" (v. 3), announced, "He is not here. He is risen as he said" (v. 6) and invited the women to look inside.

The other three gospels do not mention the Roman guards or an earthquake. Mark says as the women neared the tomb, they say the "very large stone" sealing the entrance had been rolled away. When they looked inside the tomb, they saw a young man dressed in a white robe sitting on the right side (Mark 16:5). The young man announced, "He has risen. He is not here" (v. 6).

Luke says when the women looked inside the tomb where Jesus was buried, they saw "two men in clothes that looked like lightning" (Luke 24 5). The men announced. "He is not here. He is risen" (v. 6).

John reports that when Mary Magdalene saw the stone across the entrance to the tomb had been rolled away, she immediately ran to the disciples to report that Jesus' body had been stolen (John 20:1-2). Peter and "the other disciple" returned to the tomb with her, looked at the empty tomb and the empty clothes that once covered Jesus' body, and left. Then Mary looked inside the tomb. This time she saw two angels sitting where Jesus had laid. The angels did not announce the resurrection. They simply asked, "Why are you crying." Her attention seems to be immediately drawn to a man approaching her whom she assumed was the gardener responsible for caring for the site. But when the approaching figure called her name, Mary Magdalene recognized it was Jesus.

In verse 18, she reports to the disciples, "I have seen the Lord."

That report is similar to Matthew's account. In Matthew 28:7, the angel sitting on the stone outside the tomb instructs the women to "go and tell the disciples he (Jesus) has risen." As they turned to go, Jesus appeared and greeted them (v. 9). Matthew says the women came to him and worshipped him.

What the women found that day – an empty tomb – and what they and others after them experienced – meeting the risen Lord - changed the world. From that moment forward, Christian believers have faced humankind's final enemy and asked, "Where, O death, is your victory? Where, O death, is your sting?"

The reason for such boldness? They understood that "death has been swallowed up in victory" (1 Corinthians 15:54) and that God gave victory over death "through our Lord Jesus Christ" (v. 57).

Those first Jesus-followers began to understand that "God made him (Jesus) who had no sin to be sin for us, so that in him we might become the righteousness of God' (2 Corinthians 5:21). They preached that "the wages of sin is death, but the gift of God is eternal life in Christ Jesus our Lord" (Romans 6:23). They proclaimed, "You are not redeemed with perishable things like silver or gold…but with precious blood, as of a lamb unblemished and spotless, the blood of Christ" (1 Peter 1:18-19).

That message turned the world upside down. And it still does. Being made right with God, being "joint heirs with Christ" (Romans 8:17), is not about position or power, not about heritage or resources, not about gender, race, ethnicity, or place of birth, the Christian message teaches. Salvation is open to all through faith in Jesus Christ who said, "I am the way, the truth, and the life. No one comes to the father except through me" (John 14:6).

All of that is possible only because of Jesus' atoning death and what happened next.

Dear Lord, may we add our voices to those of the women at the empty tomb to proclaim, "He is risen. He is risen indeed." Amen.

40

WITHOUT EASTER...

"Jesus...was declared with power to be the Son of God by his resurrection from the dead." Romans 1:4

Did you ever think about how the death of Jesus might be viewed if it happened without Easter?

From a purely human standpoint, Jesus' death might be seen as a tragedy. Obviously, Jesus was a gifted man. He lacked the formal training that could have made him great, the world might say, but his native ability was superior. His logic confounded the scholars. His intellect silenced his critics. His magnetism captivated the crowds. His energy carried him to the corners of Israel and beyond. Everywhere he went, people flocked to see and hear this blue-collar wanderer who walked among them as if he owned the world.

But here was Jesus hanging on a cross. His words had been too biting for some, his popularity too great. Jesus crossed powerful people one too many times. Now he was paying the price.

Only 33 years old. Imagine all he might have done had his life not been cut short by the cross, the world might reason. What a waste! Such might have been one view without Easter.

From an ethical viewpoint, Jesus' death might be seen as another example of a righteous man dying unjustly. It had happened before. It would again. Didn't Socrates drink poison rather than give in to the pettiness of the Greek court? Jesus of Nazareth was just another unfortunate example that being right is not always enough.

Jesus did nothing wrong or criminal. The Roman governor said so. Sure, he challenged some of the religious practices of his day, but they needed challenging. Sometimes he aimed strong words at the religious office holders. Remember when he said their actions were as putrid as the white stones rolled in front of the caves where people were buried?

But his words could be so comforting. Remember when he taught that the poor in spirit shall inherit the Kingdom of God and that those who mourn shall be comforted?

Jesus went about doing good. He fed the hungry and befriended the friendless. He spent time with the outcasts and guided them toward God. No one before him ever referred to the Creator God as Father, like Jesus did.

He was a righteous man, the world might say. He should not be hanged on a cross. But there he was. A man like Jesus put to death for no justifiable reason. What a tragedy without Easter.

From a political standpoint, Jesus' death shows that manipulation and intrigue can work. Bribery helped get Jesus arrested. Lies and distortions incited the crowd against him. Political threats forced the Romans to kill him. It was a deadly serious scene and it worked – without Easter.

Without Easter, the cross is merely a cruel instrument of execution. It is a sign that might makes right, that power always wins.

Jesus may not have deserved to die but once Roman power made a decision, nothing else mattered. The cross proved it. There it stood alongside the road so passersby would see the life-and-death power of Rome. The cross symbolized death. That is why the place where it stood was called Golgotha, the Place of the Skull.

That is a view without Easter.

"But now Christ has been raised from the dead, the first fruits of those who are asleep" (1 Cor. 15:20). The Bible teaches that early on Sunday morning following Jesus' death, Easter happened. The power of God the Father raised Jesus to new life, and his resurrection changed history.

One scholar wrote, "The distinctive attribute of apostolic Christianity was…the supernatural power of the living God, manifested historically by the resurrection of Christ from the dead."

Easter transformed Jesus' death from a human tragedy into a miraculous victory. Death, the last enemy, was overcome. Jesus promised, "He who believes in me shall live even if he dies" (John 11:25). As Christ was raised from the dead, so shall all who believe in him be raised. The mortal shall put on immortality. The corrupt will be replaced by the incorruptible. A new body like that of the risen Lord, a new body fit for an eternity in Heaven, awaits the believer because Easter happened.

Because Easter happened, Jesus' death was far more than a righteous man dying an unjust death. It was the righteous dying for the unrighteous. The Apostle Paul declared in 2 Corinthians 5:21, "He made him who knew no sin to be sin on our behalf that we might become the righteousness of God in him."

In other words, "While we were yet sinners, Christ died for us." Jesus fulfilled the law of God. He paid the price for the sin of all who believe on his name. He died and rose again for us.

Easter branded as a lie the argument than manipulation and intrigue took Jesus' life. "No man takes my life," Jesus said. He alone had the power to lay down his life. Jesus also said he could and would take up his life again and he did.

On the cross, a thief dying with him tried to browbeat Jesus into using his power to save the three sentenced to death. Jesus could have called 10,000 angels had he chosen. But he did not. Instead, he died for you and me.

Yes, there was intrigue and manipulation, but those smug, self-satisfied conspirators had no idea how God was working amid the evil they intended. Jesus died and rose again on Easter morning to give believers hope for today and for eternity.

The cross? It is a crude and cruel executioner's tool. But Easter even gave the cross new meaning. Easter showed the cross as a symbol of God's love. God loved us so much that Jesus became "obedient even unto death on the cross" for us. Easter made the cross a symbol of hope. The cross is empty because Jesus is not there. He has been raised.

Without Easter, Jesus death is a dark tragedy. But through the lens of Easter morning, Jesus' death is a victory over death and victory for all who believe on his name.

Yes, Jesus is risen. He is risen indeed!

Thank you, God, for Easter! Amen

ABOUT THE AUTHOR

Bobby S. (Bob) Terry is an award-winning religious journalist, having served 23 years as president and editor of The Alabama Baptist, Inc., and 20 years as editor of Word and Way, a publication of the Missouri Baptist Convention.

Bob failed his first attempt at retirement. After leaving The Alabama Baptist, Inc., he served Samford University as Advisor to the President for Faith Networks for four years.

Bob's ministry began in the local church. He served as full time pastor or on church staffs in three states. During his denominational service in Kentucky, Missouri, and Alabama, he served numerous churches as interim pastor. He has been a featured speaker in state-wide Baptist events as well as in Baptist colleges and seminaries.

Southern Baptist Theological Seminary (Louisville, Ky.) where Bob earned the M.Div. and D.Min. degrees, chose him as national president of its alumni association. Mississippi College, where he earned a B.A. degree, presented him its lifetime achievement award known as "The Order of the Golden Arrow." Bob was also awarded honorary doctoral degrees from Southwest Baptist University in Missouri and Samford University in Alabama.

Bob's leadership reached beyond Baptists. He served as president of Associated Church Press, the nation's oldest ecumenical religious press association, and as committee chairman for Evangelical Press Association, the nation's largest ecumenical religious press association. Through the years he has been active in local civic and service organizations. Currently, Bob serves on the Board of Directors for Bread for the World where he served as an officer for five years.

ALSO BY BOBBY S. (BOB) TERRY

Struggling Toward Hope:
Putting Life Back Together After a Death.

BOBBY S. (BOB) TERRY

Available on Amazon

Made in the USA
Columbia, SC
24 April 2024